Over and Over Again

OVER AND OVER AGAIN

Understanding
Obsessive-Compulsive Disorder

by

FUGEN NEZIROGLU
JOSE A. YARYURA-TOBIAS

Lexington Books

D.C. Heath and Company • *Lexington, Massachusetts* • *Toronto*

The information provided in this book is not intended to be used for treatment purposes. Anyone who has obsessive-compulsive disorder should consult a professional for diagnosis and treatment. None of the case illustrations are descriptive of a specific patient. Symptoms are often similar and, therefore, some readers may identify with a particular patient description. This is solely due to coincidence. The names of all the patients described in this book have been changed to protect their privacy.

Library of Congress Cataloging-in-Publication Data

Neziroglu, Fugen A., 1951–
Over and Over Again : understanding
obsessive-compulsive disorder / by Fugen Neziroglu,
Jose A. Yaryura-Tobias
p. cm.
Includes index.
ISBN 0-669-24997-1 (alk. paper)
1. Obsessive-compulsive disorder—Popular works. I. Yaryura-
Tobias, Jose A., 1934–   II. Title
RC533.N49   1991
616.85'227—dc20   90-49384
                                                                          CIP

Published simultaneously in Canada
Printed in the United States of America
Casebound International Standard Book Number: 0-669-24997-1
Library of Congress Catalog Card Number: 90-49384

The paper used in this publication meets
the minimum requirements of American National Standard
for Information Sciences—Permanence of Paper
for Printed Library Materials, ANSI Z39.48-1984.

Year and number of this printing:

91 92 93 94 8 7 6 5 4 3 2

Contents

Preface

I am who I am.

My illness is not me.

I carry an illness.

My illness doesn't carry me.

I am myself forever.

My illness is not.

Where there isn't home, still there is hope.

When I have no one, still I have myself.

If I fall down I will get up.

Because I will fight back.

Because each day will be a battle

that gradually I will conquer

with my own help

and the help of others.

Because I want to be free.

I want to be healthy.

Therefore, I will never give up.

Introduction

OBSESSIVE-COMPULSIVE disorder (OCD), although still unrecognized by most people, affects about six million Americans. In any given year 69 per 10,000 people will develop the condition.

Because the symptoms are so severe, OCD can be devastating. Patients often cannot maintain emotional and social relations, have difficulty coping with daily life events, and have problems studying or working. Consequently, they face emotional and economic losses.

Sometimes the disorder progresses because it is not diagnosed and therefore not treated. Sometimes the patient believes it will spontaneously go away, but it rarely does. Sometimes the patient, family, and friends deal with the symptoms in a way that is not helpful and in fact very often destructive.

With proper treatment, however, the chances of recovery are good. Treatments found to be successful include behavioral and cognitive therapy and drug therapy. Following treatment, patients can function once again. They can recover their losses and join the mainstream. Those with OCD should never give up.

Over and Over Again was written for patients and their families, their friends, therapists, and all those who are interested in individuals who have obsessive-compulsive disorder. While the book mainly addresses issues raised by patients, it will be helpful to all those involved with them, including family members, friends, coworkers, employers, and therapists.

This is a survival manual for the patient. Over seventeen years, we have learned from our patients what works and what does not. We are grateful that so many of our patients have shared with us their suffering in an open, trustful manner. Because of their experiences, we can transmit our understanding to many more OCD sufferers and improve treatment. We also would like to acknowledge the many caring families who have lived with the patients' pain. They too have contributed to the formation of this book.

Our previous book, *Obsessive-Compulsive Disorder: Pathogenesis, Diagnosis, and Treatment* (1983) was written for professionals. It gave all the scientific findings reported in the literature, as far back as the late 1800s. While this book does not cite the research literature, the text is based on scientific fact and on our own experiences.

We suggest that the book be used to answer questions raised by family members and therapists. Patients may also use this book when they feel down or are very anxious; doing so might give cause for hope.

Over and Over Again also can be used as a self-help book. Choose the chapter that is most appropriate for you; the format enables you to skip around. Reread the same chapter if you want. Perhaps you will be inspired to keep trying even if you have suffered a setback.

My compulsion is to drive with my eyes closed on the Long Island Expressway. I can drive quite a few feet with no problems.

I must confess that when you told me not to ask again whether the medication causes tremors, I began to phone my druggist and ask him the same question up to fifty times per day. Now I have no druggist. I hope you keep me as your patient. By the way, does the medication cause tremors?

Ten years ago I "took" a one-dollar bill lying on a sidewalk. How could I live with myself? I'm no longer an honest person. And by the way, don't tell me I just happened to find it, that I didn't steal it. Anyways, I should have returned it to the police.

1

The Full-Time Companion

Going Back to the Past

At the beginning, and for centuries to come thereafter, men and women were unable to explain natural phenomena, diseases, and death. How did they feel when someone died? How did they react contemplating a sunset? What was their response to a thunderstorm, a flood, or an earthquake? How did they feel when someone had a heart attack? The inability to explain it all caused fear and uncertainty. To cope with the mysteries of nature, society developed a system to appease these unknown forces. This system included magical thinking, beliefs, myths, religiosity, superstitiousness, and ritualistic behavior. With the passage of time, acquisition of knowledge delineated new frontiers among science, magic, and religion, establishing new bonds. Consequently, a common ground exists, and it can be seen in obsessive-compulsive disorder (OCD).

Ancient men and women were unable to explain the mental and behavioral changes in people. Why did a person become excitable, euphoric, enraged, uncontrollable? And then, months later, how could that same person become melancholic, unable to move, tearful? How could they understand someone who refused to eat in order to die, or someone who twitched and compulsively cursed the gods? In those days, they didn't have scientific means to explain it all, but they tried.

Some people became interested in the complexity of diseases that made their fellow persons suffer, lose their minds, or become crippled for life with chronic, painful, or devastating illnesses. These people were known as sorcerers, shamans, medicine men, magicians, and physicians. They all combined knowledge and experience, magic and beliefs to soothe the soul and repair the body. They used herbs, songs, rituals, foods, wine, music, sleep, and dream interpretation to heal the mentally ill. In this manner, magic, religion, and psychiatry became related. In modern medicine we still find a little of magic and rituals in the practice of healing.

The psychological aspects of OCD seem to have their roots in magic, superstition, religion, rituals, false beliefs, and magical thinking. In fact, a great percentage of patients are obsessed with thoughts of religious or superstitious content. In addition, patients have a tendency to abide rigidly by rules and prohibitions such as those found in religious laws. When one of these rules is broken, a ritual must be performed. As we understand it, a ritual—a highly detailed, complex act—is carried out in order to undo some obsessive thought or action that we consider inappropriate, sinful, or capable of causing damage to people or objects.

Not long ago, mental patients were declared to be demon possessed and were burned as "punishment." This horrible practice was forced on those suffering from conditions such as obsessive-compulsive disorder or Gilles de la Tourette's syndrome. Although modern societies reject the idea of demon possession, there are still certain communities or religious groups that believe in demon possession and use exorcism to expel the devil from the body. We have seen several cases of OCD and Gilles de la Tourette's syndrome that were believed to have been incidents of demonic possession.

Another factor associated with OCD is superstition. Superstition is a false belief that if something occurs, something tragic may follow. For instance, breaking a mirror, spilling wine, or opening an umbrella inside a house may lead to disaster. Superstitious beliefs are culturally determined and vary in different countries. In order to prevent tragedies from occurring, someone must perform a ritual. For instance, if someone spills wine on a tablecloth, throw salt over the left shoulder.

About 250 years ago, physicians already knew about the presence of OCD. However, it was not until the end of the nineteenth century and the beginning of the twentieth century that a better knowledge of OCD was acquired.

At the beginning of this century, OCD was considered to be mostly an organic condition, that is, a medical disorder located in the brain. Later on, it was seen as a psychological condition by psychiatrists practicing psychoanalysis. At the beginning of the 1970s, a new approach to the understanding of OCD was initiated among the professionals of the field, and new ideas developed thereafter. These include biochemical and behavioral concepts that have become fundamental for the management of the disorder.

OCD devastates the well-being of a person, reaching every corner of one's self. One loses the freedom to express one's life. OCD also affects one's emotional, physical, and social life; it reduces contact with the outside world, causing isolation and forcing the patient to live a secretive life. Although the patient wants to enjoy life, wishes to work, and mostly wishes to interact with people, the disorder disrupts daily life. Unfortunately, OCD is quite demanding. It requires continuous obedience and catering. One suffers the disorder twenty-four hours a day; life revolves around OCD with its unwanted fears, haunting doubts, merciless horrible thoughts, and exhausting rituals. All these symptoms are continuously at work; they enslave, take away hope and the future, and deprive patients of contentment and peace. OCD operates like a hurricane—leaving behind hopelessness, sadness, and enough anxiety and stress to consume one's life.

Facing such an illness, which systematically enslaves the patient, the patient is left with one option: to go for help. But this is more easily said than done. Why? At the beginning of the illness, as long as patients handle their symptoms on their own terms, there is no need for outside intervention. This coping mechanism occurs because many patients don't know they have OCD. They think their thought and behavior is right, and the world around them is wrong. For instance, a man who washes his hands twenty times a day sees this action as quite acceptable. He is clean and neat. He has strong beliefs about germs and contaminants in the environment and merely feels that society is either unaware of the germs or does not care about them; thus, others behave indifferently or irresponsibly.

It is not until patients experience intense and severe symp-

toms or when OCD begins to interfere with their daily functioning that they seek help. During the interview, we examine the
body and the mind. We look into the interaction between
patients and their families, their emotional ties, their ability to
make friends. We learn about their environment, school, and job
performance. Where do they live? How do they live? How do they
adjust to their environment? We may request blood work, brain-
wave tracing (EEG), brain radiographs, an electrocardiogram,
physical examination, and psychological testing.

We request many tests and ask many questions because getting acquainted with the patient and his or her surroundings is
basic for the design of an individual treatment program geared
to satisfy the patient's emotional, physical, and social needs.

What is the aim of treatment? We want to restore the emotional and physical balance—to remove the burden and the heavy
load that OCD puts on the patient's life. OCD creates chaos and
brings anguish, sadness, oppression, and stagnation. Patients lose
their capacity to make decisions and enjoy life. The right to be
free and in control must be restored. Treatment is not short term.
Ample time is required to heal, reshape, rehabilitate, and self-
adjust once again to a better way of life.

Definition

An obsessive-compulsive disorder is a disease of the brain manifested by intrusive, unwanted, and persistent thoughts that cannot be rejected. They keep coming back over and over again.
OCD also entails doubting, inability to make decisions, and continuous hesitation that interferes so much with life that eventually one cannot function. The patient may seek the help of others
to make decisions, thus creating dependency on others. Also,
OCD results in irresistible urges or compulsions. These urges
must be satisfied at once; an anxiety of great intensity builds up
unless the urge is carried out. Once the urge is satisfied the anxiety decreases to allow the urge again to grow stronger and stronger
and then the anxiety begins once again to build up. In this way
a vicious cycle develops. Gradually, obsessions and compulsions
become full-time companions meshed in our lives forever, unless
we decide to break off the relationship.

In addition to the three main OCD symptoms—obsessions, compulsions, and doubting—the disorder presents many other symptoms, such as the ones in tables 1–1, 1–2, and 1–3. OCD affects four main areas:

Emotional—the way we feel

Behavioral—the way we respond

Cognitive—the way we think

Perceptual—the way we perceive

Secondary Symptoms

As one patient put it, "Doc, I feel I'm cursed. I have my compulsions, tremendous fear all day long, and then I get depressed over the way I feel. It's like I can't escape." What Joey didn't know was that his other symptoms—anger, phobias, sexual problems, changes in his voice and speech, as well as perceptual disturbances—were related to his OCD. We thought by telling Joey that these other symptoms were related to his OCD, he could feel a sense of relief knowing that as his OCD improved, so would the other problems. Contrary to our belief, Joey became more upset. He wanted to know why he couldn't have another disorder with fewer complications.

Most disorders, physical or mental, do have secondary symptoms, that is, other problems in addition to the primary one. We will briefly describe some of the common secondary symptoms of OCD.

ANXIETY

Anxiety is fear of any given situation and the uncertainty of its outcome. Anxiety is a very common symptom of OCD. In fact it is so common that for many people OCD is a form of anxiety disorder. When one is anxious, one feels frightened, restless, or just uncomfortable. Physical symptoms may be sweating, tremors, butterflies in the stomach, dry mouth, stammering, headaches, palpitations, dizziness, feelings of weakness, nausea, abdominal cramps, feelings of passing out, and so forth.

Table 1-1
Characteristics of OCD

Symptoms	Compulsions	Ideational Compulsions	Motor Compulsions
Keep coming back	Mental	Counting	Aggressive
Invasive	Physical	Drawing	Physiological
Penetrate the mind	Provoke anxiety	Reviewing conversations	Rituals
Cannot be resisted	Repetitive	Repeating someone else's words	Double-checking
Useless	Cannot be resisted		Collecting
Senseless			
Repetitive	**Aggressive compulsions**		List making
	Cursing		Writing
	Self-mutilation		Talking
			Handwashing
			Watching oneself in the mirror
			Echolalia (echoing of speech in one's mind)

Self-mutilation	Physiological Compulsions	Movement Compulsions	Ceremonial Compulsions
Hair pulling	Defecating	Touching	Handwashing
Eyebrow plucking	Urinating	Tics	Showering
Eye gouging	Eating	Clapping	Housecleaning
Wrist cutting	Vomiting	Squeezing	Clothes cleaning
Body slashing	Drinking	Jumping	
	Coughing	Stretching	
	Swallowing	Throat clearing	
	Performing sexual acts	Sniffing	
		Rubbing	
		Abnormal movements of the body	
		Normal movements of the body	
		Echokinesis (movement mimicking)	
		Lip smacking	
		Spitting	

Table 1–2
Important Symptoms in Obsessive-Compulsive Patients

Symptom	Percentage
Depression	94
Anxiety	90
Aggression	65
Dysperception	60
Phobias	58
Double-checking	55
Other rituals	54
Sleep disturbance	49
Family disturbance	45
Washing excessively	41
Sexual disorders	34
Appetite disorders	33
Meticulosity	27
Self-mutilation	16
Tics	1

Note: The percentages given above were compiled from the authors' files.

DEPRESSION

Depression is a feeling of sadness accompanied by a loss of drive and joy of life, feelings of hopelessness, helplessness, confusion, and inability to perform. Physical symptoms such as general weakness, insomnia, excessive sleepiness, extreme tiredness, fatigue, exhaustion, headache, loss of balance, constipation, loss of appetite, loss of weight, and loss of sexual desire may be present. In addition, suicidal thoughts and moodiness may be common. Symptoms of depression may switch to symptoms of aggression. The depression we see in our OCD patients is usually the result of their inability to control the symptoms that dominate their lives. They feel very frustrated. The depression rarely precedes the onset of OCD.

AGGRESSIVE BEHAVIOR

We see three types of aggressive behavior in our patients: mental, verbal, and physical.

Mental aggression consists of having violent thoughts that are

Table 1-3
Primary OCD Qualities

Thoughts	Behavior	Mood	Mode of Activity	Social Aspects
Doubtful	Ritualistic	Anxious	Repetitive	Inability to function
Intrusive	Repetitive	Depressed	Hesitant	Family disturbance
Magical	Bizarre	Angry	Slow	Inability to work
				Difficulties while working
				Inability to make friends
				Inability to date
				Inability to maintain emotional ties with others

not obsessional. That is, they can be controlled by the patient and repelled from the mind.

The verbal manifestations of aggression consist of yelling, shouting, or cursing.

The physical manifestations of aggression are directed toward people or objects. When they are directed toward people, they are usually limited to the family. It is common to find aggression and/or anger in OCD patients. In one of our studies, 65 percent had at least one type of the mentioned aggression.

PHOBIAS

A distinction has to be made between a patient who has a phobia and one who has OCD with phobia. Patients with a phobia can control it by avoiding what they fear, while patients suffering from OCD with phobias must engage in rituals in order to control their phobic symptoms. For example, a phobic patient who is fearful of snakes can avoid snake-infested areas. A phobic patient fearful of elevators can use the staircase and avoid the elevator. However, a patient with OCD who is phobic of Acquired Immune Deficiency Syndrome (AIDS) must wash every time he or she thinks the AIDS virus is present. Merely avoiding sexual contact with an AIDS patient is not sufficient.

It is important to differentiate between a phobia of germs and the phobia seen in an obsessive patient. A person who suffers from a phobia of germs will try to avoid germs. The person who suffers from obsessive phobias of germs thinks of germs all the time.

SEXUAL DISTURBANCES

Sexual disturbances are commonly seen in obsessive-compulsive patients. Symptoms include an increase or decrease in sexual desire, frigidity, impotence, and delayed or premature ejaculation. Most often these disorders are originated by the patient's rigid viewpoints on moral or religious matters and/or fears of contamination. Of course, if it is owing to the latter, then it is not a secondary symptom but a problem directly resulting from the primary problem (OCD). Many patients suffering from OCD need to analyze, and perhaps even overanalyze, important matters. Therefore, they continuously modify their attitude on sex. Sometimes the sexual disturbances we observe are the side effects of medication (see chapter 7).

SPEECH PATTERN

Speech is one important way to communicate with the outside world. The speech of OCD patients may offer clues to diagnosis and predict the outcome of their illness.

When OCD patients talk, they are tangential — never to the point — repetitive, circular, circumstantial, and redundant. Their tone of voice goes from a high to a low pitch. In addition, we can observe changes in the speed of the speech. They may speak extremely fast, in order to catch up with the speed of their own thoughts. Some patients are extremely verbose, that is, they have a compulsion to talk constantly. In fact, they may become extremely irritable if anyone dares to interrupt them. In other patients, we sometimes observe extreme preciseness in their speech, with excellent diction.

Two qualities of speech are noticeable: patients usually speak in the first person pronoun and in the past tense. Patients with OCD rarely speak about the present or the future; they usually speak about themselves, showing their unavoidable self-centeredness. If you carefully listen to their speech, you will find a great amount of explanation and a lot of negatives.

PERCEPTUAL DISTURBANCES

Nearly one hundred years ago it was noted that some patients complained of visual changes, such as the presence of floaters or transient spots in front of their eyes. Just several years ago we noticed that our patients reported seeing objects in their peripheral vision, such as books falling from a shelf, objects falling from their pocket, or an animal walking by. Usually we ask patients about these occurrences. Rarely will they report it on their own. This visual dysperception usually forces patients to double-check in order to reassure themselves that nothing has occurred.

Diagnosing OCD

It is sometimes difficult to diagnose OCD. OCD involves many different symptoms that may overlap with symptoms seen in other emotional disorders. The two most significant examples are anxiety and depression.

If an OCD behavior is extremely bizarre, OCD may look like schizophrenia. But the reasoning in the OCD patient is always *intact*. A patient may be *unreasonable* but never *irrational*.

CLASSIFICATION OF OBSESSIVE-COMPULSIVE DISORDERS

It is important to know as accurately as possible what kind of OCD we are being confronted with. We say it is important because a good diagnosis will lead to a good treatment program and, consequently, to a better outcome. We usually classify OCD into three main groups: the primary or simple form (the classical OCD that we are talking about in this book); the OCD with phobic symptoms; and the unusual obsessional patient. The following classification will help you to understand this condition better.

Medically Induced Obsessions and Compulsions. A side effect of some medications may be obsessions and compulsions. We have observed these side effects following the administration of chlorpromazine (more commonly known by the trade name, Thorazine).

Obsessional Conditions. Long ago another form of OCD was described as a condition characterized by a moody personality. This condition resolves itself very quickly.

Manic-Depressive Form. Some patients suffering from OCD may have a manic-depressive component. That is, patients with OCD may go into a manic stage characterized by mind racing, excessive physical energy, no need to sleep, no need to eat, grandiosity, very fast speech, hesitation, anger, and so forth. Patients fluctuate between being manic and being obsessive-compulsive. This appears to be an uncommon form. Perhaps if this OCD were studied more closely, however, it might not be considered rare. This condition can be easily treated by administering lithium. We cannot confuse this condition with the side effect of some anti–obsessive-compulsive agents that may cause a manic response within the first two to three weeks of treatment. In that case, the discontinuation of the anti–obsessive-compulsive agent will bring an end to the symptoms.

Habits

Habits are learned behaviors or customs. They develop gradually and become routine. An example would be putting a wallet in the right inside pocket of your jacket. Habits may become automatic, subconscious, and even involuntary. In fact, we might not be aware of some of our habits, such as hair twirling, nose rubbing, nail or lip biting, finger tapping, gum chewing, thumb sucking, or doodling.

Habits are not the same as compulsions. A compulsion is a voluntary act that must be performed; otherwise it causes anxiety. We are always aware of our compulsions.

Habits might be present in patients with OCD. Having various habits doesn't mean you have OCD, however. One behavior or one symptom does not make an illness or disorder.

Other Disorders

Here is a list of disorders where OCD may be present:

Schizophrenia

Manic-depressive illness

Hypochondriasis (obsessive concern with one's health)

Hysteria

Anxiety disorder

Depression

Mental retardation

Epilepsy (seizure disorders)

Parkinson's disease

Encephalitis

Three years ago I changed the complete electric outlet of the ceiling in my dining room. I am obsessed with the idea that I put it in incorrectly and that a short circuit may cause a fire. This idea came to my mind one year ago. You should also know I sold the place two years ago. I have attempted to obtain authorization from the new owners to come in and check the outlet. They have reassured me that everything works fine. I insisted and they have threatened me with the police if I don't stop harassing them.

I wash my hands out of fear of germs.

I wash my hands to be clean.

I wash my hands, but I don't know why.

I wash my hands because they are always sticky.

2

The Turning Point

O CD patients often perceive their symptoms as invaders from outer space. These unwanted invaders change the course of their lives.

Carmen

Although she was a premature baby with jaundice and at age four she fell off her bike and was unconscious for a few minutes, Carmen was a healthy young girl. Nonetheless, at age seven she became restless, constantly moving around, always on the go. Not even her favorite television show could keep her sitting still. At night she refused to go to bed, insisting she could do with little sleep anyway. Her short attention span was noticed in school, where her behavior had also become quite disruptive. She talked in class, teased her friends, and overall, created havoc. Her school called her parents in. A psychological consultation was followed by a referral to a child psychiatrist. The diagnosis was hyperactive behavior, nowadays known as Attention Deficit Disorder. Carmen was put on tranquilizers and improved considerably. Six months later she was a normal kid who brought joy and pride to her parents.

At age nineteen, as soon as Carmen got into college, things changed for the worse. Two years later we met Carmen for the first time. Although her college grades were excellent, her marks were slowly declining. She was insecure about her knowledge; thus she would read over and over the same chapters of her textbooks, almost to the point of memorizing them word for word.

She approached all her school material the same way. One doubt always arose in the middle of a task, whether it was eating or watching a movie. "Do I know enough to pass my exams?" The answer was always the same: "I don't know." Then at once the urge to stop whatever she was doing surfaced, and she immediately went back to her books to study more.

Sometimes she tried not to give in to her compulsion to study, but it was useless. She would begin to sweat under her arms until her blouse was soaked. More antiperspirant had little effect on it. Her hands became clammy. The solution was to open a text-book and study. That did it. Her stomach distress, sweating, and "uptightness" would disappear. Once her obsessions and compulsions invaded her brain she was forced to give in to her compulsions.

How many dates did she lose because of her sudden departures, such as leaving a guy in the middle of the dance floor? How about when her parents invited her to a Caribbean resort, a dream vacation for her, and she ran away from Kennedy Airport before boarding the plane? She couldn't go; she had to study. Step by step her OCD was moving in, waxing and waning here and there, but gaining ground. The battlefield was already there, the healing war still to be uncovered by Carmen, who thought of herself as a dedicated student, highly driven and ambitious, a symbol of success. Her parents were highly pleased with Carmen's achievements. Unknowingly, Carmen's parents were partners in her illness. Inevitably, things were going to deteriorate, quite rapidly in fact.

One morning in February, she decided that reading her text-books over and over again, taking notes, and attending lectures weren't going to solve her problem—to learn and know everything. Because her need to be in control, to know everything, became stronger each day, she modified her strategy to study. "How about if I copy everything I read in my books?" Carmen said, and the mere thought of getting to know more made her smile. She began to copy everything like an old scribe or copyist.

That decision was the turning point in her life. Most of her time was dedicated to writing, and time to eat and to sleep was reduced to a minimum. Carmen was unable to go out, visit her family, and so forth. One day she realized that she could no longer obsess with being knowledgeable. She then realized she didn't want this kind of unreachable goal. Perhaps something was wrong with her. Soon after these thoughts came to mind, she realized how poorly she was doing. Then she failed sociology, the subject in which she was best prepared. She had failed for the first time. She couldn't cope with her life. So an anxious, depressed, confused, frightened, and abandoned Carmen consulted us.

We met with Carmen and her parents. We told them of the relationship between Carmen's birth and her OCD. Although premature babies do not always develop OCD, some patients have a history of birth problems. Was jaundice a factor? It's hard to tell. But the fall at age four was something to consider. In fact, Carmen's hyperactive behavior developed two years after the fall. Hyperactivity is frequently found in those who have OCD. Then we explained the need for blood and urine tests. We also requested a five-hour glucose tolerance test, which looks into the ability of the body to burn excessive sugar. Burning more sugar than necessary could signal a low blood-sugar condition. Low blood sugar causes fatigue, anxiety, irritability, nightmares, insomnia, and dizziness, among other symptoms. We also explained the need for a brain-wave test, or EEG (electroencephalogram). Some patients with OCD have an abnormal EEG. These findings can be seen in other conditions as well, but if the results of an EEG rule out a seizure or convulsive disorder we can select medications that won't trigger a seizure or convulsion. We spoke about the need for psychological testing and the possibility of having a personality study done. Once we gathered the material requested, we met again with Carmen and her parents to discuss a program suitable for Carmen's needs.

The blood and urine tests were normal. She did have an abnormal sugar test, which showed below-normal sugar levels. The brain-wave test was normal, as were the personality tests. We confirmed the diagnosis of obsessive-compulsive disorder and discussed the possibility of a cure. We gently explained that OCD is a chronic disorder. Some patients sustain longer periods of remission. Others never have symptoms again. We could not predict what would happen in her case. Therapy aims to restore functions, making Carmen a useful individual. We could also help her to graduate so she could make a living and have a family if she so desired. Treatment included the use of anti – obsessive-compulsive medicines for at least six months because these drugs don't show immediate effect. It takes at least two months to see some results. One of our psychologists took care of her behavioral treatment.

Between four and five months later Carmen began to show signs of improvement. In the meantime, she followed a diet high in complex carbohydrates and low in refined sugars with a good amount of proteins. Within a year she was back in college as a full-time student. After eighteen months she was off medication, although she needed further behavioral therapy.

Carmen became a successful lawyer. She's still quite a reader and note-taker as well as an achiever. She is a hard worker, but no longer is she a patient with OCD. Now Carmen is in control.

What is a symptom? When we sneeze we tell ourselves we're catching a cold or that hay-fever season is here again. An upset stomach or nausea brings about thoughts of possible food poisoning. These symptoms or signs warn our bodies that something is wrong. In a way, symptoms are messengers of our insides. Cough, pain, fever, and fatigue are some types of physical symptoms, whereas nervousness, shaking, confusion, anger, and loss of sleep are mental symptoms. Obsessive-compulsive disorder has many symptoms. Sometimes these symptoms are also present in other mental disorders. This makes diagnosis of OCD sometimes rather difficult because it can be mistaken for other conditions.

Mr. Doubtful

One major symptom of OCD is doubting. Doubting is an uncertainty about the reality of our beliefs or actions. Consequently, we cannot make decisions. This was true for Herbert, one of our patients who was well acquainted with doubting.

"I knew about your clinic for the last two years. As a matter of fact I made an appointment for a consultation three times and I had to cancel them all." This was how Herbert introduced himself at our first meeting. Doubting was his most severe symptom; he was nearly incapacitated by it. At age thirty-eight, separated, with two children he was unable to support, he had moved back into his parents' home. His doubting had made him dependent on others, especially his wife. His wife—as he told us—could no longer put up with his continuous demands to clean and to make decisions for him. "I need a husband and the children a father, not this vegetable," his wife said.

So Herbert went back to his parents' house and played the role of son. His parents were in their late seventies. How could they take care of his life? Herbert regressed to a ten-year-old in a child/parent relationship. "Are you suffering from OCD?" we had asked him on several occasions. "Who knows?" he would reply, although he exhibited many OCD symptoms.

"Perhaps, I don't know, how can I be sure, I have to check on that one, I am not certain, let me think about it, who knows, well . . ." were some of his typical replies when we tried to diagnose his condition. Certainly, doubting was a main drawback for Herbert. This symptom was going to jeopardize his treatment. Would he make up his mind and come for treatment?

At this point Herbert's family became a very important and irreplaceable factor in Herbert's treatment. Without their moral and economic support, chances of recovery were slim. He had no friends, and his one sibling lived in California. Obviously his social resources were limited. He was placed on an anti – obsessive-compulsive agent and underwent a program with strong psychological intervention focusing on three main targets: to improve his sense of inadequacy, to understand the nature of his many symptoms, and to develop a sense of certainty.

Herbert's treatment was long and painful because he was unable to adhere to treatment. He couldn't follow treatment as indicated because he would become quite irritable. We told him not to call on the phone thirty times a day to be reassured that there was nothing wrong with something he had done. He eventually followed our order but then began to call someone else instead. So in a way, he was cheating in therapy. That was painful.

Sometimes we expect patients to cheat on the treatment because it becomes unbearable to hold so much anxiety inside. So if they have urges, they have to let them out and try to satisfy them. In Herbert's case he fulfilled his urges by making repetitive calls to be reassured.

While Herbert was in therapy, his wife filed papers for divorce. That, of course, brought further anxiety and overwhelming insecurity that drove him to the point of becoming almost nonfunctional. Because he was still in therapy, however, he could be helped through his crisis. Sedatives brought some relief to his anxiety. Gradually he began to make small decisions. Step by step he became encouraged after proving to himself that his decision making did not cause the pain, anguish, or sense of failing that he expected. He also realized that sometimes failure was not so horrible. He was better able to accept life's situations and demands, and he learned how to adapt to different circumstances. He also began to see the positive aspects of any situation, no matter how bad it appeared.

In Herbert's case, the psychological intervention was crucial in teaching him how to be assertive. In addition, we used some behavior therapy, since Herbert had many other OCD symptoms. For instance, he checked and double-checked his list of a million and one things. He had a need to count nearly everything because he feared missing things. But the main symptom that overshadowed everthing else was doubtfulness, the target symptom that we tried to control and eventually did.

Gradually, he improved and became his own self. Once again he felt reassured, secure, and extremely adequate. He moved out of his parents' house, improved his social network, and finally established a very good relationship with his children, who loved him very much. Every weekend was a time of joy for all of them.

The "Touch Your Navel" Compulsion

We've forgotten his name but not his symptom: an irresistible urge to touch his navel. Everything started when he was six years old. One day, out of the blue, he touched his navel, and thereafter he could not resist the urge to touch it over and over again. Many years later, a psychoanalyst explained to him why he touched his navel. "Something to do with my Oedipus complex and my tremendous attachment to my mother. I didn't remember well but all I knew was that the explanation was not clear enough," he said.

This patient also had obsessions and other compulsions. However, the main reason to see us was his urge to touch his navel. That urge caused him a lot of problems at work, a busy supermarket, where he was the manager. In order to touch his navel he had to unbutton his shirt and slightly lower his trousers. Because this behavior became noticeable, he made holes in all his shirts so he could touch his navel without being so obvious. If he resisted the impulse to touch his navel, he would become extremely anxious and begin to perspire, his hands would shake, his heart would race, and he would become so confused that he couldn't perform as a manager. In order to relieve himself of this tremendous anxiety, he would put his finger in his shirt hole while talking to employees or customers. This cost him his job. In his particular case, behavioral therapy was of great help. The patient was trained not to touch his navel. Concurrently, other intense compulsions were treated. The "touch your navel" compulsion was completely suppressed within four months.

The Collectors

We have all collected, saved, and hoarded at one point in our lives. And Sam wasn't different from the rest of us, except he favored a strange kind of collecting: his nail clippings. Twenty-five years of nail clippings had been neatly saved and stashed away in his attic. We said neatly because each individual nail clipping was glued to a cardboard sheet, in which the date of the clipping was carefully printed with Gothic characters.

What about Jean's collection? She collected everything from clothing to safety pins. Her house was full of items. "You never know when you may need them," she used to say. Yet fashions change and magazines or newspapers may be retrieved from libraries or computerized files, but how many safety pins can you use in a lifetime? Trying to reason with her was beyond hope. Her husband attempted to stop her from collecting, but whenever he tried, Jean became outraged, her anxiety level skyrocketed, and the marriage moved closer to collapse.

Jean could be easily understood by Joey, whose house was a maze of piled-up used radios of every year, brand, and model. Because he was interested in nostalgia items, he began to collect radios as a hobby. Gradually, he filled one of the bedrooms that was no longer used after his children moved out. He then began to place radios on shelves and in the hallways. Eventually he invaded his living room, dining room, and his own bedroom with radios. He did the same with the double-car garage and had to remove his car. Eventually his wife's car had to be moved from the garage to the driveway because the whole garage was clogged by radios. To be precise, he had collected 578 radios.

At age thirty-nine Martin came for a consultation. He was a file clerk in the warehouse of an old publishing house. For the last fifteen years he had been saving garbage and his own feces. For that purpose, he managed to buy a house surrounded by a garden so offensive odors could be kept away from neighbors. Once in a while when he thought he had collected excessive garbage or feces, he would dispose of them. He confessed he couldn't handle his anxiety had he thrown out garbage or feces every day. He couldn't get rid of his own excrement because that meant burying himself alive. For those who think he was irrational, let us tell you that he wasn't; all his psychological tests showed him to be quite a rational person with severe symptoms of obsessions and compulsions. In Martin's case, a behavioral therapist had to go reluctantly to his house to help the patient get rid of all the collectibles. Yet what intrigued us most was his obsessiveness with fear of contamination! After six months of intensive behavioral therapy and medication, however, Martin improved considerably.

What makes people save or hoard unnecessary things no matter how bizarre the items are? Is it stinginess? Is it greed? Is it fear of losing it all? Is it that urge to have so that we will feel safe? Is it one way of protecting our future? And if so, how and why? These are questions to be asked of those who save even their money for food, accumulate goods, and consume little. Sam, Jean, Joey, and Martin belong to a different category. Obviously the items they saved are useless and bizarre. All of them realized how crazy it was to behave this way, but they admitted to their inability to give up these strong compulsions.

The Twitch and OCD Connection

Cynthia was a fifteen-year-old student when she came to see us for the first time. Her symptoms were facial tics, twitches, hissing, and a compulsive rubbing of her nose. Her tics were mostly blinking and the production of funny sounds. She was told that her tics would go away because they were just a regular occurrence of childhood. In fact, her pediatrician incorrectly thought she suffered from childhood tics. When the tics became intense and disabling, her parents took her to a psychiatrist, who diagnosed her problem as Tourette's syndrome. But Cynthia came to see us because of severe obsessive-compulsive symptoms in addition to her twitches. She had to dress and undress compulsively for about three hours every morning; consequently, she was always late for school. Cynthia then began to get up at about 4:00 A.M. so she would have time to ritualize. She couldn't tell us why she had to ritualize.

As her problem worsened, a new ritual appeared: crossing back and forth over the threshold of her bedroom. This ritual took from twenty minutes to two hours. Ultimately, her life became a nightmare. She ended up in a children's psychiatric ward, where she was given several medications, among them haloperidol. On this drug her tics improved considerably, but her obsessions and compulsions did not. By the time we saw her she was obsessed with thoughts of her parents' deaths as well as her own. Then she realized she performed her rituals to prevent her parents from dying. The magic in her life was assuming a predominant role that was damaging one of the most important periods of her life: adolescence.

Cynthia's mother, Louise, was a real estate broker in her forties. She could hardly work because of her migraines, phobias toward chemicals, and inability to make decisions. Her father, Peter, a fifty-two-year-old general surgeon, was a violent man who used to beat his wife.

Louise's indecisiveness was evident from the way their house was furnished. There were no beds, only mattresses, and the living room was empty. A small table and a few chairs were the only other pieces. There were few ornaments on the walls.

Was it true that Cynthia was raped by her father at the age of eleven? We knew very well the difficulties involved when she

came here with OCD symptoms. Could we treat her successfully
without treating her entire family? Could we inquire thoroughly
about the sexual abuse that took place? We tried to progress
gently, but to no avail. Once the family was confronted with their
past, they chose another facility.

Prisoners in Their Homes

Three patients — Jackie, John, and Mel — came to the clinic at different times, but we found similarities in their case histories.
Their family lives had all been seriously disrupted by their
illnesses.

Jackie, twenty-seven years old, was obsessed with germs and
contaminants present in her house. Gradually, she became preoccupied with germs outside the house, waiting for her in public
toilets and sinks, on doorknobs, floors, restaurant utensils, and
supermarket foods. She protected herself against germs by washing her hands. Her handwashing was excessive; in fact, she would
wash them over 100 times a day. Her hands were rubbed so raw
that a skin graft had to be performed. When Jackie came to see
us for the first time, she walked into the office with her hands at
shoulder level, her arms flexed at the elbows and covered with
white gloves. "Is there anything red here? I hate red, red is blood,
and I hate blood," she said.

Over the previous few years she had made a fortress of her
home, keeping doors and windows tightly closed. A good air con-
ditioner provided her with the necessary ventilation. In addition
to her washing rituals, she spent eight hours a day systematically
vacuuming the house and its contents. When Jackie rented an
oxygen tank so she could survive in her contaminated surroundings, her parents gave her an ultimatum. Either she would seek
treatment on her own or they would commit her to a mental institution. Here some clarification is needed. During the previous
two years Jackie had rarely gone out of the house and had refused
to seek professional help. Her family had contacted us, and for
about one year we kept in touch, but to no avail. Somehow Jackie
managed to control her parents' lives. Her father was an accountant in Manhattan and had to commute daily, while her mother

was a retired teacher carrying the burden and responsibility of Jackie's care. The mother, like her daughter, became a prisoner of OCD, whereas the father was a prisoner on parole, serving time in the community. They came to us asking for help, grasping for freedom and expressing a bit of hope since Jackie had decided to try treatment.

John was twenty-four years old when he completed college. He had married Susan while still in school. Susan developed melanoma, a malignant cancer of the skin, and died within six months. Her death demolished John's life structure, dreams, happiness, love, and thoughts of togetherness. John became lost in his own sadness and in the chronic mourning that he could not control. Tears welled up in his eyes whenever he thought of Susan. He was alone, and he feared the loneliness of his bed and the terrifying moment of waking up in the morning to find no trace of Susan "even in the pillow or the blanket."

Somehow John managed to graduate, and he went to work in a bank. He started planning to obtain a degree in business administration. Friends and relatives assumed he had recovered. John had hope and felt at peace with his changes. He faced a new beginning with new challenges. For the first time in a long time, life seemed promising. But then he had a horrible nightmare in which Susan told him he couldn't be happy because her departure should be mourned forever. He then resumed his grieving. He sank into a sea of obsessions and could hardly keep afloat.

John felt drawn into a whirlpool of anxiety. Frightened and unable to cope, he became depressed and despondent. He became drawn and sunken-eyed, he lost weight and cried frequently. Because he was plagued by insomnia, a night of uninterrupted sleep was cherished. He lay awake at night, obsessed with his past. One night he tried to resist his obsessive thoughts. He rearranged the furniture in his house, keeping everything in symmetry. He nailed pictures on the wall at the same height and distance. These tasks helped to rid him of his obsessions and to reduce his anxiety level.

Eventually the depression reappeared, and John gave up. He couldn't face the world: it was too tough. New York was no place to meet people; you just became part of the rat race. Within three months he was unable to leave his house, though he wanted to go out and keep his job. Finally he got used to the idea of being alone in his house all day. He either sat for hours contemplating the walls or stayed in bed. He couldn't read, listen to the radio, or watch television. His parents brought food once a week, but John allowed them to stay no more than half an hour. His apartment was spotless and symmetrically arranged.

One day he ran out of food because his parents went on vacation for two weeks. He didn't eat for about a week. He was taken to a hospital emergency room, dehydrated and confused. It was there that our first encounter took place.

Mel was a forty-two-year-old divorced father of three and successful medical scientist. He would ride to his office in midtown Manhattan at 6:00 A.M. Upon arriving he would fix himself two cups of black coffee without sugar, eat a bagel with cream cheese, and then light his first cigarette. Next, he would tackle the dozen or so scientific articles that were neatly stacked on the right side of his desk. By 8:00 A.M. he would finish his reading. The rest of his daily routine included laboratory work, a midday tuna fish sandwich, teaching, writing, and more reading. The day ended at about 8.30 P.M. He had worked like this six days a week for the last seventeen years. Was he a workaholic? Not only was he a workaholic, he was also a perfectionist, a methodic, and a high achiever. Despite his wisdom, however, he couldn't foresee that after his second cup of coffee on May 15, life would never be the same.

He opened the front drawer of his desk, looking for the draft of the paper he was writing. It had taken two years to produce what was probably a breakthrough, and he was proud of it. But the paper wasn't there. Mel searched through the other drawers; it wasn't there either. Mel called his secretary and asked his associates, but there was no trace of the paper. Was it in the computer? He looked for the floppy disk but couldn't find it. Perhaps it was misfiled and would show up later. Well, if he had to he could use his raw data and rewrite the whole thing.

The next day, as customary, he started to make his coffee. The coffee can was there but not in the usual place. "That's funny," he said to himself. He took a puff of his cigarette, opened the first drawer of his desk, and voilà! the paper was there. Overjoyed, he proceeded to work on it.

Within a short time, however, Mel sensed that at least part of the paper seemed to have been written by someone else. He dismissed his thought as a crazy idea. Next day, Mel had the feeling someone had broken into his house. For one week he felt as if someone was in his house when he was at work. So he started to bring his work home and spend more time there with the hope of catching the intruder. Did he go to the police? "They'll think that I'm nuts," he said to himself.

One afternoon Mel looked out the window of his office and thought that someone was watching him with binoculars. He shut the blinds. Too many things were happening to him: the missing research paper, the possible intruder, and finally the feeling of being watched through binoculars. He instructed his secretary to keep the venetian blinds down and his office door shut at all times. Later he installed a double-bolt lock and an alarm system in his apartment.

Finally, Mel said, "Someone is after me." One morning he refused to leave his apartment and for years thereafter he remained incarcerated there, vowing to protect himself and prevent his work from being stolen by another scientist. He became angry and nasty. His only contact with the outside world was his brother, with whom he had a rather stable relationship. His brother was there for him when he divorced and now he needed him again. But no one on earth, not even his brother, could persuade him to seek help. "Just once, please, go and see a psychiatrist," his brother pleaded week after week.

Mel would leave his apartment only to fulfill his basic needs. He might go to the dentist or shop at the grocery store across the street. Ultimately, he exhausted his savings because he had no disability insurance. Since he refused to be examined by a doctor, he was ineligible for such coverage.

When we examined him, Mel was in very bad shape. He was emaciated, extremely nervous, very guarded, uncommunicative, and uncooperative. He was poorly groomed, and his sadness showed in his face. It took quite a few sessions to break through his defenses and gain his trust. Eventually, we diagnosed him as suffering from a paranoid syndrome. Mel had misinterpreted many incidents. His ability to make judgments had so badly deteriorated that he was unable to reason. Consequently, he withdrew from the world and felt persecuted. He did have an obsessive-compulsive personality, but that was not the reason for his inability to function. We persuaded him to take medication. Within two months he began to show signs of improvement. Eventually, he was able to function, but at a different level. Unfortunately he never regained his status as the reputable scientist he had been.

Jackie, John, and Mel led different lives, yet they all had a common denominator: they were homebound. They all had obsessive-compulsive symptoms. Jackie suffered from OCD and stayed home from fear of contamination; John became so depressed that going out became unbearable; and Mel was so paranoid he could no longer see the world realistically, rather he saw only a world ready to get him.

Sometimes paranoid symptoms are seen in patients suffering from OCD. When this occurs it becomes difficult to distinguish one condition from the other. Because the brain is the union of billions of cells with different activities to perform, and because all these cells are united through thousands of circuits, it's no wonder that when a break in the circuit occurs, the brain begins to work improperly. As a consequence, symptoms associated with different diseases may overlap, producing a confused picture. This is why obsessive-compulsive symptoms are often mixed with depression, anxiety, or paranoid symptoms at times.

Prisoners of Their Appearance

Mike, twenty-one years old, had not gone to school on a regular basis in his last two years of high school and, since graduation, had worked only sporadically. He had spent the last four years in his home. If he did leave his house it was at night to ride around and to get a glimpse of life. Mike lived with his parents and two sisters, although no one in the family noticed his presence. Mostly, he remained in his room and at times came out for dinner. If anything, he was an embarrassment to his sisters, who were afraid their boyfriends would wonder why their brother didn't work or date. How could they explain that their brother thought his jaw was too pointed and his hairline too imperfect to venture out? How could they tell them that Mike spent hours applying various hair products and looking at his jaw in the mirror? If he were to come out while their friends were around, Mike would probably look at his reflection in the silverware or in the glass oven door. In fact, Mike spent the majority of the day looking at himself or watching television. He didn't want anyone to see how ugly he was, even though no one else thought he was unattractive.

Mary Lou was not very different from Mike. She obsessed about her body and face shape. For years she had thought that she was ugly and that everyone stared at her. She hid her body behind big, bulky clothes, and her face was seldom seen by anyone but her parents and one brother. She would have preferred to live alone and not be noticed by anyone, but she couldn't afford her own apartment. Her brother tried to introduce her to his friends; contrary to Mary Lou's self-image, he thought she was quite attractive, and on the few occasions his friends did see her, they thought she was a knockout. But there was no way to change Mary Lou's mind. By the time we saw her, she was thirty-two and had been secluded since age eighteen.

James was forty and had been living in an apartment on his own for the last ten years. His parents had urged him to seek help, but they were unsuccessful. They felt helpless; their son deteriorated each day. James's care was in their hands. They paid for his few clothes, his food, and the apartment he never left. James thought his forehead was too large and didn't want to be seen by anyone.

All the above had *dysmorphophobia*—a normal-appearing person's fear of being unattractive or repulsive to others. Many of these individuals become secluded and are unable to work or formulate interpersonal relationships. All three patients were treated with an anti–obsessive-compulsive agent and behavior therapy with varying degrees of success.

The Hypermorals

While most of us try to live a decent, moral, and ethical life, we don't frequently find ourselves tortured with doubts about our morals. We often make decisions about right and wrong and don't give it much thought. We don't question our moral judgments. Some OCD patients are plagued by their thoughts and behaviors. They believe they have behaved improperly or sinfully. They become overly concerned with thoughts, words, or deeds that they believe to be bad, wrong, and/or unethical. They have a compulsion to correct these thoughts or actions.

Robin was fifty, a happily married, religious woman. Sometimes while having sex with her husband she would fantasize about other men. This distressed her greatly. She would try to resist the images of these other faceless men but she couldn't. She would stop in the middle of sexual foreplay and pray ritualistically to ward off such thoughts. Her husband reassured her that fantasizing was perfectly natural and not the same as being adulterous. Yet she couldn't stop thinking that she was immoral. She decided not to have sex with her husband until she could stop the fantasies.

Twenty-two-year-old Fred belonged to a college fraternity. He was always wondering if he had said something that hurt his fraternity brothers. He would ask if he had and then apologize profusely, just in case. Fred was also plagued by his conscience for having stolen a chocolate bar from the local stationery store when he was seven. Although he had been told by his family that children do these things sometimes, Fred could not forgive himself. To add to his worries, he recently found out that he had unknowingly flirted with a married woman. She had picked him up in a bar, but a week passed before he was told that she was married. Since then, he blamed himself and obsessed about God's punishment.

Blasphemous thoughts entered Lillian's mind. Sometimes when she thought of God, prayed, or went to church, she thought negatively about her religion. Lillian believed her bad thoughts might be caused by years of Catholic school upbringing, but her friend Harriet evidently had similar thoughts in the synagogue. In fact, Harriet, who was friendly with her rabbi, barred him from visiting her house because of her anxiety about those negative feelings. She loved and respected the rabbi, yet she couldn't explain her negative thoughts about him.

Both Lillian and Harriet thought they were bad people for thinking negatively about sacred places or religious men. They spent hours obsessing about it and could not forgive themselves or dismiss the thoughts.

All the people above illustrate *scrupulosity*. Scrupulosity was discussed in Catholicism as early as the twelfth century. It refers to hesitation in deciding what is right. Obsessive-compulsive patients who suffer from scrupulosity, or hypermorality, have doubts about their moral judgments. They experience tremendous anxiety about acts or thoughts that they consider immoral.

The Hair Pullers

Kathy was only four, and most of her hair had been pulled out. Ten-year-old Lisa had also pulled out most of her hair by age six and had continued the compulsion for the past four years. Both were wearing wigs to the initial interview. Robert, thirty, had no eyelashes and Jill, no eyebrows. All of these patients had a form of OCD known as *trichotillomania*. Patients with trichotillomania have a compulsion to pull out their body hair. They may pull out their eyebrows or eyelashes, the hair on their arms, legs or head, and even pubic hair. Most of them are women, but we don't know why. Sometimes they report they are not aware of doing it. If you ask them to observe themselves, however, they can immediately tell you when and where they are doing it. The urge to pull may come at any time, and they believe they have to give in to it despite the embarrassment.

Jill would leave her desk at work and go to the ladies' room to pull out her eyebrows. She had devised a perfect system. She would take a compact mirror into the stall and pull out the top hairs first and work down so that it would not be so noticeable. Initially, she pulled haphazardly, but her eyebrows began to look bizarre. Then she used the mirrors in the bathroom, but the fear of being discovered increased her anxiety and exacerbated the compulsion.

Robert's compulsion was not as noticeable to his coworkers. But three years ago, a woman he was dating asked why he had no lashes. He decided that would be his last date.

Kathy and Lisa were not yet socially affected. They were limited, though, because they couldn't swim in the summer or play rough for fear their wigs would fall off.

We treated the children through behavior therapy. The two adults responded to an anti – obsessive-compulsive drug and behavior therapy. All four showed improvement and controlled their compulsions.

Alone in the World

"I don't know whether I am here or not, whether you are the doctor. Actually I feel that everything in the world is unreal except for myself." Jonathan B. looked attentively at my reactions to his words. At age twenty-four this postgraduate student of mathematics had had a promising future. But in the last year or so he had become concerned with his own existence. "Am I alive?" he constantly asked. He also grew deeply interested in philosophy and poetry. For him, life became absurd, without meaning. He became pessimistic and lacked the motivation to study. Jonathan's need to progress and achieve made him an excellent student; yet he was unsatisfied, frightened, and confused. Why? Doubts about who and what was real became overwhelming. He always thought he was the only real thing alive. The rest of the world was just a product of his imagination, a painful dream from which he couldn't awake. Jonathan used to say that he was unaware of the presence of minds other than his own. He was clearly in search of his identity and could neither feel nor experience others' identities.

In 1897, F.H. Bradley, a British philosopher, described what is known as solipsism, a philosophy that subscribes to the belief that nothing exists beyond oneself. We have encountered at least three other solipsists suffering from OCD. This finding, rare as it may be, is masked by other OCD symptoms. One patient, forty-two-year-old Charles, used to go to extremes trying to experience the presence of others. He was very argumentative and oppositional; his relationships were frequently quarrelsome. One day, he smashed his car against a telephone pole, risking his life in order to prove to himself that he existed. He was uninjured, but the presence of the rescue team, the police, the fire department, and the public was not enough to elicit a sense of being among others. An obsession develops when an individual relentlessly questions his or her existence, the meaning of that existence, and his or her identity.

The Body Checkers

We are all concerned with our bodies, and rightfully so. They are irreplaceable. Today there is a genuine interest in improving our physical and mental health, and this is a welcome attitude. But some of us are much more concerned about our bodies than others; quite frankly, some become obsessed. They're always checking their weight, pulse, or temperature. They listen attentively to any clues that may signal the onset of disease. How's my body doing today? Is this enough urine? How many bowel movements is the norm? Some people check for blemishes, scars, pimples, or skin color changes day after day. Others check constantly for tumors on their bodies.

Elaine began to check for body tumors at the age of twenty-two. Routinely, she would start touching with her fingers or the palms of her hands every inch of her body, looking for tumors. In a highly ritualistic fashion she would start from her scalp and move down to her toes. Her back was checked by a family member. At age forty-five she developed breast cancer, but she failed to detect the tumor herself. It appeared on a mammogram. Although she had surgery, Elaine's obsessional fears remained. She became preoccupied with her bowel movements and the presence of blood in her stools.

The shifting of symptoms in OCD is common. One can be obsessed with fears of germs, then of chemicals, then of AIDS, and so forth. The content of the obsession changes, but the obsession as such remains. Compulsions change in the same way. For two years a compulsion to count may be replaced by a compulsion to double-check.

Behaviorists aim to teach a method to eliminate all obsessions or compulsions. In the teaching process, however, they may select current symptoms to work on. The biological psychiatrist aims to suppress the symptom, regardless of the content, with medications. It seems that the best approach to treating OCD is to combine several forms of treatment.

The Walking Pain

Sometimes the onset of OCD appears as a single symptom, such as pain.

Peter, a twenty-nine-year-old married Navy lieutenant, was discharged from the service because of a severe emotional disorder. Two years prior to his discharge he had developed a generalized pain. This pain was dull, sharp, intermittent, continuous, excruciating, shooting, dartlike, and even superficial at times. The pain could start anywhere in his body and radiate to various parts. He went from doctor to doctor, and hospital to hospital. He took many laboratory tests and bought hundreds of prescription medicines in a futile effort. There was no physical explanation for it, and he was told he would be better off consulting a psychiatrist. So he did.

Peter has a condition known as *topalgia*, a generalized pain coming from an obsession. Peter was obsessed all day long with his pain. He was an irritable person, was extremely meticulous, and could not tolerate mistakes—his own or anyone else's. He had compulsions to check and collect used pencils and empty boxes. But nothing matched his concern for his pain. In his search for a cure, he went from talk therapy to hypnosis, from tranquilizers to antidepressants, trying everything but electroshock. Could his pain be a trick of his imagination, or was it real?

The knowledge of the medical profession is limited. Technological progress is not enough to explain everything that occurs in the medical arena. What is the cause of Peter's illness? How do you treat it? What is the outcome of the disorder? All are common questions of everyday medical practice. Peter would certainly fall in the category of a difficult patient: someone whose diagnosis is beyond our knowledge, and someone whose treatment is limited by our insufficient tools. It took us over six months to improve his symptoms. We used an anti – obsessive-compulsive medicine and a form of intensive behavior therapy. He was supported, reassured, and guided throughout his suffering. He was given instructions so he could perform within manageable boundaries. In Peter's case, the intensity of one symptom — his pain — prevented us from seeing the hidden picture of a person with OCD.

Compulsions are urges that must be carried out; otherwise anxiety builds up. This is very important to bear in mind, because the compulsion comes first, and then the anxiety, and not the other way around. As we shall see, this is a useful concept for treatment.

Compulsions can be divided into ideational and motor. *Ideational compulsions* are performed within one's mind. These compulsions include the need to count, to repeat without speaking aloud what someone else is saying, to draw pictures in our head, and so forth. A *motor compulsion* requires the activity of our muscles.

Here are four case studies to illustrate how thought, behavior, mood, and social aspects are affected by compulsions.

Pervasive Compulsions

George, thirty-five, was watching a political program on television one Sunday morning. He was quite interested in the program because he was a professor of political science at a nearby college. Suddenly, he was stricken by the urge to go to church. He hadn't gone to church in years, but for some unexplainable reason, he had a need to go that day.

Weeks went by, and he gradually became concerned with religious matters and with reviewing his past. He concluded that he was a sinful person. Although he was unable to pinpoint what sins he had committed, he still felt sinful and believed he should be punished. He began to attend daily Mass. His religious thoughts became stronger. They would frequently appear in his mind with such intensity that he was unable to teach as he used to.

One morning while shaving, George had an image of throwing one of his children out the window. The thought horrified him and made him extremely anxious. He canceled all his morning appointments and went straight to church to confess this horrible thought. The priest reassured him that it was just a thought, that he was not a criminal, that he loved his children, and that he would never do anything to hurt them. This wasn't good enough for George. He kept thinking about it but couldn't rid himself of it. Other ugly thoughts began to creep into his mind and make his life intolerable.

One afternoon while engaged in his obsessions, George began to tap his desk. He noticed that if he tapped twenty times, the thought he held would eventually leave. Tapping brought relief to his miserable days. Therefore, he began to tap every time any horrible thought came to mind. This ritual counteracted his obsessive thinking. While at times it was successful, at other times he had to count up to one hundred to repel the thought effectively. Actually, the thoughts always came back, but he believed that the tapping or counting up to one hundred would keep his children from harm. Still, George believed he was a sinner who did not deserve to be happy or enjoy life.

Ryan was a recent college graduate who returned home to look for a job. One afternoon while looking for the want ads in the Sunday newspaper, he read the news about a house that caught fire. He began to think that his house could also burn down. Thereafter, he became obsessed with the idea of a fire starting in his house. He began to double-check the furnace outlets, cigarette butts, and matches. He never said anything to anyone in the house, but he started to collect all matchboxes and got rid of them. He installed a fire alarm in each room and took courses on fire prevention. Finally, he spoke to his parents and siblings to address the issue. He suggested having fire drills as they do in schools and hospitals. He decided to have a fire drill once a week with the participation of his parents, brothers, and sisters. They went along with it. When Ryan decided to implement a fire drill on a daily basis, the family realized that something was wrong with him. They pointed out to him that he was always talking about fire engines, flammable substances, types of fire extinguishers, fire prevention, and the like. They noted that matches couldn't be found anywhere in the house and that there were too many smoke detectors. He had even put extra detectors in each room, just in case one of them failed to pick up a smoke signal.

Arguments and fights about the fire issue became part of the family's routine. Ryan became extremely violent and left the house. Two days later he returned home feeling sorry and promising to seek psychiatric help. He didn't keep his promise. Instead he refused to leave the house because he felt his family's skepticism would surely leave the house vulnerable. He felt it was his duty to stay in the house all day to prevent the possibility of fire.

Rosemary was a twenty-nine-year-old homemaker with two children. One afternoon while preparing dinner, she felt her heart beat, and she became quite interested in the beat. She thought, "Why wasn't I ever aware of my heart beating before?" But after a few days she lost interest and forgot all about it.

Five days later, she began to pay attention to her breathing, her brain, and the movements of her body. She was also extremely concerned with her bowel movements and urination. Slowly she developed quite a few physical symptoms. She became obsessed with her body functions and with her ability to perceive movements, heart rate, breathing frequency, and all those functions we take for granted.

Most of us don't think of the way we walk, how many steps per minute we have to take to cover a mile, in what way we move our legs forward, in what way we balance our arms to keep our body in good posture while walking, and so forth. Yet Rosemary was so obsessed about these things that she couldn't function without long interruptions. So she went to a doctor for a general checkup, and, as suspected, the checkup was negative. But the results didn't discourage her from consulting a second doctor, then a third, and a fourth. She consulted every available medical specialist in her quest for a cure. After two years of continuous consulting, a doctor suggested she see a psychiatrist. Rosemary certainly suffered from an obsessive-compulsive disorder, with her body being the main obsession.

A patient suffering from obsessive-compulsive disorder carries a chronic conflict: the inability to choose between believing or not believing in the obsessions. This conflict occurs even though obsessions are basically useless and endless.

Thirty-eight-year-old Bob was a married father of two. Most of his life he had worked as an electrician. He became ill with OCD at the age of twenty-one. One of the main symptoms of his illness was to double-check the work he had performed. Every time he finished a job, he repeatedly checked his work, no matter how small the job. When asked why, he said he was afraid of the possibilities of causing a short circuit or of someone being electrocuted. Because of his intense urge to double-check and his inability to stop it, the time invested in each job became longer and longer. Eventually, double-checking interfered severely with his performance. He was unable to keep appointments with his customers or to perform major jobs because he needed about half a day just to install a couple of electrical outlets.

Compulsive Rereading

Some patients engage in reading the same paragraph or even one single sentence over and over again. At times, this type of reading behavior may affect and jeopardize academic performance. Students suffering from compulsive rereading may have to quit school altogether and give up their aspirations.

At the age of thirty-four, John was completely homebound. He was engaged in compulsive housecleaning that could take up to sixteen hours a day. Housecleaning also included dishwashing, a task he performed by hand. Interestingly, John would wash one plate with his left hand and dry another one at the same time with his right hand. The most outstanding feature of his illness was that he was illiterate. When I asked him why he didn't know how to read and write he told me that he went to first grade and he became stuck on the first line of his reading book. He could not stop rereading those first few words the teacher taught at the beginning of that year.

Retracing

Some patients have the urge to go over things they have previously performed. For instance, a person who writes a letter and has the need to rewrite on top of the words is an example of a retracer. There are patients who have the need to retrace steps; if they walk in a certain direction, then they have to walk back in the opposite direction by stepping on their invisible footsteps. This may also be done in reading, as we have already seen.

Throughout our many years of having been in contact with patients suffering from OCD, we have gathered information on an incredible number of behaviors and symptoms. These collections have become our main sources of knowledge for diagnosing, treating, and researching this illness. Looking back in our files, we found two cases that, although hard to believe, were nonetheless true and involved retracing steps. One of the two patients came to our facility from across the country. He came by car because of the impossibility of returning to his home by retracing his steps backward from our center, to the airport, to the same plane, same seat, and so forth. After his interview, he left our office by walking backward toward the exit. At the same time, another patient who had the same problem was entering the office by walking backward, and they bumped into each other. Both knew they were suffering from the same disorder.

Sometimes all the compulsions mentioned here may be performed repeatedly and without any specific purpose, or at times they may be performed to undo or prevent disastrous consequences.

Sexual Obsessions and Compulsions

OCD can also affect the sexual life of the patient. Two known obsessive and compulsive activities include nymphomania (excessive sexual desire and activity by females) and satyriasis (excessive sexual desire on the part of males).

Compulsive masturbation is also common. This may be observed in children who are neglected and/or rejected, or in adolescents suffering from depression. Compulsive masturbation has even been reported in infants, accompanied by rocking and head-banging. This behavior usually occurs before sleep.

Compulsive exhibitionism is also characterized as OCD, and manifests itself as an intense urge to expose one's sexual organs to the public. Obsessive concern with shape and size of genitals is another OCD symptom. Women obsessed with the size of their breasts may resort to surgery to decrease or increase breast size.

Obsessions of being homosexual or the urge to touch or stare at the genitals of the identical sex may be present in a male or female heterosexual. Occasionally, sexual aberrations or perversions may also be compulsive.

Maybe I am blind. So I close my eyes to see whether I see or not, but when I open my eyes, I think they are closed. So I close them again, feeling that now they are open and perhaps they are not. So I open them again, feeling that they are closed.

I have doubts, perhaps I am right. You might even be a dream. Things are getting worse. I doubt others are alive. I know it sounds crazy, but I can't help it. This obsession of being the only living thing on this earth haunts me day and night.

When I come to your office, I leave home three hours in advance, though I only live twenty minutes away. I like to be on time.

3

Journey to the Unknown

How Does It Begin?

EARLY ONSET

Jim, a six-year-old, was on his way to school. Suddenly, he decided to touch a picket fence with his hand. At first he touched every single picket. Then he began to touch every other picket. Another child has a need to skip over cracks on the sidewalk. Both of these activities are some of the solitary games of childhood. This type of game eventually disappears. Nevertheless, some children develop the urge to touch a picket fence or to skip over sidewalk cracks, and they can't continue walking without carrying out the urge. This innocent game may indicate the starting point of a compulsive behavior. This behavior is characterized by the urge to carry out an act while intense anxiety builds up. Once the task is performed, one feels immediate anxiety relief, until the urge reappears and the same task has to be performed over and over again. Urge and performance walk hand in hand.

Joann consulted us about her intense need to be clean and live in a spotless house. She was a homemaker in her mid-thirties, and her main chore in life was to clean constantly. She could be found cleaning the kitchen floor at 1:00 A.M., even if she had to get up very early in the morning to get her children ready for school. Going back to her childhood, she recalled her mother taking her, impeccably dressed, to play in the park, even though she was going to play in the sandbox. Nonetheless, her mother would even carry along shoe polish and a cloth in order to keep her shoes shining.

Mary was a twelve-year-old bright student who always had to have the last word. Since age seven, every time she kissed her parents good night she always had to be the last one to speak. If her parents said "good night, Mary," she had to add something else immediately, otherwise she couldn't go to bed.

These are just a few examples of how OCD may start. In the first example, Jim doesn't know the origin of his compulsion. In the second example, it appears that Mary has learned her compulsion from observing her mother's own cleaning compulsions. In Mary's case, there is no apparent reason for the onset of the illness.

Instances of OCD commencing during childhood comprise approximately 30–40 percent of reported cases. Keep in mind that compulsive behavior is normal in children. These traits appear at age two and may last four to five years. Compulsive behavior seems to be a response to an individual's need to control his or her environment. As patients grow older they might adhere to repetitive patterns of behavior. These patterns are seen in eating, washing, and dressing habits. Children convert these patterns into rituals. If this period of compulsive behavior persists, OCD develops.

In observing children with OCD, one finds parental demands as a precipitating factor. Parents often order their children to be neat, organized, clean, and so forth. This is not always the case, however, nor does the presence of a precipitating factor indicate that it is the cause. Children's symptoms are sometimes very similar to those of adults.

Compulsive behavior in children becomes more evident around bedtime. Children become repetitive in words and actions. They may say good night repetitively; they may undress and dress several times; they may fix bed linens or touch objects in a particular manner. In most children, these rituals disappear in time.

In children suffering from OCD, these rituals never leave spontaneously; they remain the same or worsen. Eventually, these rituals will interfere with daily functioning. It is important to remember that children know their behavior is alien or abnormal. Consequently, they try to fight their symptoms, but unless they are instructed, their fight is futile.

The following characteristics were found among children with OCD:

1. compulsive movements (entering or exiting repetitively, moving their heads, touching)
2. compulsion to sit, get up, or move at the right time (they sense when it is right)
3. sudden onset of symptoms
4. above-normal intelligence
5. combination of obsessions and compulsions
6. obsession with fear of contamination
7. perfectionism
8. disruptive behavior at home and school
9. adult-like moral code
10. rigid thinking (stubbornness)
11. active fantasy life
12. no symptoms of psychosis
13. no symptoms of mental retardation
14. anger and guilt

Obsessive-compulsive behavior can be seen in autism, childhood depression, childhood phobias, fire-setting, Gilles de la Tourette's syndrome, organic brain damage, and childhood schizophrenia. Childhood OCD, if untreated, will become adult OCD. Although symptoms, course of illness, and treatment may differ, the illness is generally the same for both children and adults.

Most serious symptoms of OCD appear during the early twenties. It usually takes about seven years from the onset of illness to seek professional help. This gap indicates that either OCD develops subtly and slowly or that the patient is embarrassed or too frightened to come for consultation. In general, patients come for treatment when the illness is well advanced or when they are unable to function.

EARLY ONSET

At age twenty-four, Jim found himself sitting in the kitchen, unable to function. Each of his movements had to be recorded in a notebook. He was obsessed with muscle control and with his brain commanding his body to move. He could rest only lying in bed or sitting in a chair.

When Jim was fourteen, he found himself washing excessively because he felt the world around him was a pigpen. He took pride in the order and neatness of his bedroom. He never completed college because he had to read the same chapter over and over again. He had to be certain that he remembered everything.

For the last six months Jim had been caught in this business of having to record all his movements. Anxious, unable to stop all these urges, he sat alone, in sadness, finding emotional and economic support only in his elderly parents. If they died, then what?

When Margaret got a good job at the industrial plant fifty miles from the Canadian border, everyone was happy. In times of unemployment, she felt lucky to have a job. Margaret was a timid, bright, orderly person with a strong drive for perfection and achievement. Becoming an assistant manager opened the door to success. Yet she had a drawback: in order to perform she had to have the "right thought." The right thought had to be positive and pleasant. As long as she had negative, unpleasant thoughts dwelling in her mind, she couldn't perform. One bright morning, on her way to work, she found herself having unpleasant thoughts. Therefore, when she reached the corner where she always turned to go to the factory, she couldn't do it; she had to keep on driving. Because her house was near the Canadian border, she found herself driving toward Canada. Fortunately, a good thought came to mind, and she was able to turn around and go to work. Thereafter, and for one year, she found herself driving to work, having unpleasant thoughts, and at times having to cross the

Canadian border because she was unable to think positively. The severity of her symptoms forced her to carry an overnight bag in case she got stuck in Canada with negative thoughts. All alone, she managed to keep her behavior a secret. But she ran out of excuses to justify her absences at her place of work. Ashamed and frightened, she finally went for help.

LATE ONSET

Ronald was a happily married, sixty-year-old grandfather who had just retired. He had been a compulsive hard worker. A six-day workweek and a short vacation here and there defined his drive to accomplish. He never left a task unfinished. As a self-employed person, he liked to be his own master. Ronald was forced to retire, however, when he suffered a major heart attack. After being discharged from the hospital, he found himself dwelling on illness and death. Then a serious compulsion developed: He had to check just about everything. Faucets had to be tightly closed. The same went for windows, drawers, and doors. But the worse compulsion was to check for cracks in the house. The house was almost forty-five years old, and cracks were abundant. He became depressed, he cried, he lost his appetite, and he refused to leave the house.

OCD may manifest itself at an older age. It is usually seen in persons with obsessive-compulsive traits or personality. One of the precipitating factors is retirement. Retirement brings with it many questions about life and its purpose, as well as a fear of aging and death. At this time OCD can surface as a result of a crisis, as it did in Ronald's case.

Are You Suffering from OCD?

The following is a list of symptoms that may appear in an OCD patient. It is important to note that one symptom does not make an illness.

Saving newspapers for many years

Handwashing more than ten times per day

Double-checking lights every night

Removing fingerprints from any visible surface

Clipping articles

Tapping your night table top several times at night

Doodling while talking on the phone

Making sure your shoelaces are symmetrically tied

Always being on time

Being a perfectionist

Being highly moral

Being a worrier

Being doubtful

Being unable to make decisions

Overanalyzing everything

Organizing compulsively

Making lots of checklists

Questioning repetitively

Not tolerating sloppiness

Having a very clean kitchen

Hating dishes in the sink

Making the bed before leaving the house

Having difficulty tying your shoes

Dressing and undressing

Having an inability to tuck in your shirt

Having "magical" thinking

Being superstitious

Wiping down the shower door after taking a shower

Diagnosis is not a label but a procedure applied to identify, clarify, and make a disease more understandable. Without a diagnosis or with a wrong diagnosis, treatment is bound to fail. Diagnosing—calling things by their rightful name—is not labeling. Labeling patients is interpreted as putting a stigma on someone suffering from an emotional disorder. We don't label patients; we label goods. But we certainly give a diagnosis in order to obtain the best available treatment. If you are not satisfied with a doctor's diagnosis and recommendations, remember that you are always entitled to a second opinion.

Am I insane? OCD is not insanity; it is a disorder in which, on most levels, reason is preserved. Patients live within a real and whole world. It is true that, at times, symptoms are extremely bizarre, even senseless; obsessions can be strong and merciless, and those afflicted may dwell on abhorrent thoughts of manslaughter, sexual aberrations, religious sins, or crimes that a "normal" being would never dream of entertaining. But these obsessive-compulsive ideations are never carried out. Patients are aware that their beliefs and feelings are abnormal. They fight symptoms; they want to be cured, and they are not insane.

Rose was in her twenties and spent most of her time in the bathroom. For about eight hours each day she engaged in rituals of handwashing and showering. She also had the urge to splash water on the walls of the bathroom and to dry the walls and floor once the rituals were completed. This type of behavior began several years earlier and gradually increased in time and performance. She dedicated her life to ritualizing, and consequently she couldn't work. She had been homebound for over a year. Her family became concerned with her bizarre behavior. They wondered who in her right mind would spend all day in the bathroom washing her hands and body and splashing the walls with water. A psychiatrist was consulted, and a diagnosis of schizophrenia was made. The patient underwent intensive therapy with tranquilizers and antidepressants. Medication appeared to be ineffective, and the patient deteriorated rapidly. She became angry and experienced outbursts of violent behavior during which she would break objects and verbally abuse her family. Occasionally, she went into bouts of deep depression. All along, her compulsions to wash and to splash water remained unchanged. By this time, eight years had elapsed from the onset of her illness. Finally, psychosurgery (operation of the brain) was recommended. The surgery was followed by a recovery phase that lasted about four months, after which the symptoms recurred.

This is one of the unfortunate episodes that may occur when a patient is misdiagnosed. Rose had been diagnosed as schizophrenic because her behavior was extremely bizarre. Unfortunately, no one ever realized she was aware of her strangeness. She *was* in contact with reality. She didn't want to give in to her urges, but was unsuccessful in fighting back. Her sense of awareness of being ill, her normal judgment and ability to reason, plus her inner reality did not fit the criteria for a diagnosis of schizophrenia.

Quite often, the way symptoms are presented may lead the psychiatrist or psychologist to a misinterpretation of the information obtained, and thus a wrong diagnosis is made.

In one of our studies, we found that from a sample of one hundred cases of OCD, a previous diagnosis of OCD was made in only twenty-four cases. Of seventy-six wrongly diagnosed cases, sixteen were diagnosed as schizophrenic. In addition, since most patients have severe symptoms of anxiety and depression, these symptoms not only mask the presence of obsessions and compulsions, but they may also lead the professional to miss the diagnosis of OCD.

Richard was a twenty-eight-year-old married man who came for a consultation because he had recurring episodes of depression. He had been hospitalized twice and even underwent electroshock therapy when drugs failed to relieve his depression. He was an electrical engineer working in a supervisory capacity at a factory. Now he was uncertain whether he should go to work. He had been married for the last two years. Since age fifteen he had been unable to make a decision. When he was single, his decisions were made by his parents. He was extremely dependent on his mother. His inability to decide was destroying his life. How should he choose a career? Where should he go on vacation?

Now he was married, and his wife was in charge of everything. He blamed his wife for any mistake. Obviously he failed to realize that his wife made unilateral decisions because he couldn't make them. Even when he went to the supermarket to buy milk, he was unable to pick one of fifty available cartons.

Richard's marriage was shaky. He didn't know whether to have children. He felt overwhelmed, unable to be in control. Life seemed worthless. He was depressed and fearful. He was unable to function as well as before.

Because of doubting or the inability to make decisions, many patients lose their freedom to choose, and they must rely on others to make decisions. Usually, a family member becomes the thinking and decision-making brain.

Richard suffered from such intense depression that unless he was examined thoroughly, the diagnosis of OCD could have been easily missed.

Is OCD a fatal illness? OCD kills no one directly. Patients with OCD may have suicidal ideas, or even suicidal gestures. Suicide is rare among patients with OCD.

Am I dangerous? OCD does not make a person homicidal. Obsessive thoughts of violence are not carried out. A small group of patients may self-mutilate. Self-mutilation consists of cutting, pressing hard against sharp objects, pricking, burning the skin, hair pulling, nail biting, and mouth-wall biting.

Did I inherit OCD? There is no definite answer to this question. Few research protocols are being conducted to investigate genetic factors. We may say, though, that 8 percent of patients have parents with OCD. Some genetic ties between OCD and Gilles de la Tourette's syndrome have been reported.

Did I catch OCD? OCD is not a transmittable disease. It is not contagious. There is no direct proof that it comes from viruses. But it might be related—in some cases—to viral encephalitis (an inflammation of the brain).

Is my upbringing the culprit? In the homes of patients with OCD, anything is possible. Anxiety, fear, depression, and anger among family members are known to exist. OCD certainly may be learned, and this should be taken into account before outlining a treatment program.

Who is most vulnerable? No one is particularly vulnerable. Anyone may develop OCD.

I cannot tolerate mistakes made by me, or even others.

I have only spoken the necessary words during the last two years, because I must pronounce and space my words in a perfect way. If I don't, I become very anxious. I stammer, I stutter. I may go a month without saying a word.

I wear a ring on my left pinky finger. I wear a ring on my right pinky finger. One watch on my left wrist, one watch on my right wrist. The same goes with my pockets. Symmetry is important to me. Balance is important to me. Weight has to be well distributed on my body.

4

Partnerships

T HERE are other conditions that interface with OCD. These conditions have their own uniqueness, yet they all have symptoms of obsessions and compulsions.

Self-injury

Eating disorders

Compulsive Orectic Mutilative syndrome

Gilles de la Tourette's syndrome

All four conditions show physical and mental symptoms, clearly indicating a close interrelationship between body and mind. In all of them, the body is affected by one or more factors: self-injury; distortion of the body image; severe weight changes; or body twitches or tics. Although these conditions are not truly OCD, their obsessive-compulsive symptoms require us to address the use of OCD therapeutic techniques in addition to the customary treatment programs of that particular condition.

Patients usually try to injure areas that can easily be concealed from others. The removal of eyes or genital parts is seen only in severely psychotic patients.

Self-injury can be part of OCD. We have found it in about 15 percent of one sample population. Treatment includes behavioral and drug therapy. The most difficult patients to treat are those suffering from hair pulling (*trichotillomania*), primarily when hair pulling is the only or most important symptom.

Self-Injury

Self-injury is the voluntary harming of one's bodily parts, primarily the head, face, and arms. The following list shows the types of self-injury:

Wrist cutting

Skin picking

Skin burning

Skin scratching, to the point of bleeding

Eye removal

Genital injuries

Hair pulling

Tongue biting

Cheek biting

Lip biting

Knuckle biting

Eating Disorders

Bulimia (eating binges followed by vomiting) and anorexia nervosa (a refusal to eat accompanied by menstrual changes) are the main eating disorders. In bulimia and anorexia nervosa there is a need to be perfect (such as perfect body shape) or an urge to obtain pleasure and gratification, whereas compulsive eating may be a way of distancing oneself from other people or not having to deal with one's sexuality.

THE MAIN CONCERNS

Patients suffering from eating disorders are primarily concerned with two factors: body shape and food intake.

Helen, a twenty-one-year-old college student, had a strong urge to eat everything in sight. She would binge mostly on carbohydrates. In one sitting, she could go through half a loaf of bread with peanut butter and jelly, a piece of cake, several cookies, and some ice cream. Afterward, she would feel so guilty for having eaten so much that she would force herself to vomit. Two fingers in her throat or a couple of glasses of water would do the trick. She would promise herself never to eat like that again, but the urge to binge would reappear and the process would start all over again.

As time went on, Helen found herself leaving parties to go home to binge. She prayed for her roommate not to be there because no one knew about her problem. She always binged and vomited alone. She was of normal weight, and except for her peculiar eating habits, no one could guess her problem. Her friends thought she was a picky, strange eater. In front of them, she would take small portions, push her food around with a fork, and slowly eat her serving. She was usually choosy about her food selection. At times, food would inexplicably disappear, half a jar of jelly, for example. But no one made too much of it.

As Helen's binges increased (as do most compulsions), the only way to control her weight gain was by vomiting. Gradually, she began to feel very bad about herself. Bulimics usually have very low self-esteem and are self-deprecatory and perfectionistic.

Behavioral treatment of bulimics is similar to that of true OCD patients. They are exposed to their favorite foods, asked to eat, and prevented from vomiting by careful monitoring. They are asked to let friends, or at least one friend, know about their problem. By doing so, they have someone to eat with who can prevent them from vomiting. If vomiting can be prevented, then normal eating is eventually resumed. In patients suffering from bulimia, other issues such as depression, perfectionism, extremely high need for achievement, assertiveness, social skills, and development of intimate relationships have to be dealt with.

Martha was a thirty-five-year-old secretary who weighed three hundred pounds. Throughout her life she had been obese. Her weight gain became noticeable after she was raped at the age of fifteen by her uncle. She became afraid of men. She was an extremely beautiful woman, and she blamed her rape experience on her beauty.

Therefore, she unknowingly resorted to compulsive eating to destroy her sexual attraction. She lived in isolation, without friends. Most of her eating would take place in bed, at night. I pointed out to Martha that it seemed she'd rather have food in bed than a man. She said, "Yes, food is my lover." Once a treatment program was handed to her she said to me, "I won't follow your treatment because I couldn't be unfaithful to my lover." I never saw her again.

I met Eileen when she was twenty-two years old, a medical student who was severely depressed and who had attempted suicide by overdose at the age of seventeen. She was extremely bright and resourceful in order to be a medical student and function as such, despite her emotional turmoil. She weighed eighty-nine pounds. She hadn't menstruated since age sixteen, when she began to lose weight. At that time, her weight was 120. She was a worrier, checking everything in sight. She always felt obese. A hardworking student, she managed to maintain good grades and made it into medical school. But the intensity of her obsessions with food made her life miserable and resulted in severe bouts of depression. Because she ate with her family, and later on in the school cafeteria, it was very difficult to refuse eating. As she put it, "I always have people witnessing what I eat." Yet she managed to eat minimally, primarily vegetables. She also resorted to laxatives and vomiting to lose weight. She would take up to twenty laxatives a day and exercise compulsively. Finally, she could no longer hide her condition. Her whole life had become one ritual over food.

The obsession with eating, food, and body weight and the compulsion to eat or not to eat may have different explanations for each individual. Following are rituals commonly seen in eating disorders:

Weighing food

Preparing food

Carefully selecting food

Cooking procedures

Eating in an unusual manner

The way patients handle food and their eating habits are revealing of the obsessive-compulsive nature of their symptoms.

PRIMARY ANOREXIA NERVOSA

Anorexia nervosa is a condition characterized by self-induced weight loss, loss of menstrual cycle, and psychiatric symptoms. Following are other characteristics:

Onset before age twenty-five
Loss of over 25 percent of original body weight
An urge not to eat
A phobia toward food
Body-image distortion
Body growth of thin hair
Slow pulse or heart rate
Hyperactive behavior

Compulsive eating and vomiting (episodes)
Obsessions
Compulsions
Loss of menstrual cycle
Aggressive behavior
Sexual dysfunction
Insomnia
Family constellation disturbances

Will lack of food hurt my body? Lack of food will hurt your body, as happens in any other condition where starvation is present. The whole body will suffer tremendously, as you can see in the following physical symptoms:

Brain atrophy
Swelling of the legs
Loss of muscular mass
Bone growth in the joints
Yellowish tint to the skin of the palms
Liver damage
Loss of fatty tissue

Infections
Loss of teeth
Stomach distress
Bowel dysfunction
Low levels of vitamins
Lack of vitamin A
Loss of menstruation
Thyroid conditions

Is anorexia a uniquely female condition? Not always. Male cases of anorexia nervosa have been reported, although these cases are uncommon.

Is anorexia nervosa related to OCD? As far back as 1939, researchers have drawn similarities between anorexia nervosa and OCD. Patients display obsessive-compulsive behavior. They are obsessed with food and complain of an urge to eat. They are obsessed with their body shape and ritualistic preparation of food. If they don't give in to their compulsions to eat or not to eat, anxiety builds up.

What is the cause? No definite or single cause of eating disorders has been established. Important factors are depression, perfectionism, phobias toward food, family disturbances, and severe perceptual distortion of body image.

Biochemical theories have included a dysfunction of the hypothalamus—a cerebral region intimately associated with our emotional balance. Abnormal biochemistry involving neurotransmitters has been mentioned as another factor contributing to anorexia nervosa.

What are the chances of recovery? The outcome of treatment depends on the length of the illness and severity of symptoms.

Poor family relationships and angry behavior will seriously reduce the chances of a favorable outcome. In addition, there is a group of patients who display hysterical behavior. These patients are very angry and extremely moody, tend to act out, and are unable to follow treatment. If they ever improve, they will immediately sabotage treatment until they worsen again. Patients with severe obsessive-compulsive symptoms also have a poor prognosis, unless these symptoms are specifically treated.

Can someone die from anorexia nervosa? Going into starvation is dangerous and can be fatal. The mortality rate of the anorexic population reaches up to 30 percent.

TREATMENT FOR ANOREXIA

Treatment for anorexia nervosa varies according to the therapist's beliefs. A psychologist will choose a psychological approach (analytical, behavioral, cognitive, or family therapy), while a biological psychiatrist will use medications (antidepressants, anti–

obsessive-compulsive agents, or cyproheptadine [Periactin]). Ideally, a joint approach would be more comprehensive and successful.

Compulsive Orectic Mutilative Syndrome (COMS)

COMS affects only women. During Phase I of COMS the patient is anorectic and amenorrheic (does not menstruate). During Phase II, after the anorexia phase is terminated and menstruation returns, the patient self-mutilates and exhibits aggressive behavior. Throughout both phases obsessions and compulsions are present.

The cause of this disorder is not known. The various physical symptoms — mainly menstrual changes, aggression, and an eating disorder — may indicate a brain dysfunction, probably related to a glandular condition. The psychiatric symptoms of anxiety, anger, compulsions, and obsessions may be linked to a biochemical disturbance.

Following are some of the characteristics of COMS:

Obsessions

Compulsions

Aggressive behavior

Self-mutilation

Elevated pain tolerance

Menstrual changes

Eating disorder

Insomnia

Family disturbances

COMS presents in two phases, the first characterized by a refusal to eat; an urge to avoid food; a compulsion to eat and vomit; and an abnormal menstrual cycle. After the menstrual cycle returns, Phase II appears, characterized by aggressive behavior and bodily injury. In both phases obsessions and compulsions are present.

Elly, a twenty-five-year-old woman, came for a consultation visit. She had developed anorexia nervosa at the age of fifteen. She grew up in a violent family setting where she was physically abused. Unless she weighed eighty-five pounds or less, Elly hated herself. Fear of gaining weight forced her to rinse some of her food to prevent any ingestion of oil or fats. She was hospitalized twice for starvation, and she gradually became more and more anxious and depressed. By the age of twenty, Elly was a very angry and depressed person; however, she had put some weight on, begun menstruating again (something she had not done since she was fourteen and a half), and even entered college.

One night, for no apparent reason, Elly began to squeeze her skin until it bruised. Then she took a razor blade and cut herself. During the ritual of cutting, she did not experience pain. This behavior continued for years; after four hundred cuts or so, she came for help.

Except for her neck, Elly's entire body was cut. She had to dress in long sleeves and slacks to cover her wounds. After undergoing three years of psychoanalysis and two of regular psychotherapy to no avail, we proposed a program of behavioral therapy, with family participation, and an anti–obsessive-compulsive drug. After six months of treatment, the self-mutilation stopped. Eventually, Elly graduated from college, married, and had a child. Five years later she was doing well, without further treatment.

Gilles de la Tourette's Syndrome

Tourette's syndrome is characterized by motor (muscle) and mental symptoms. It is more common in males. Symptoms appear early in childhood, beginning with excessive blinking. This is followed by facial twitching. Gradually, twitches may move downward and affect arm, abdomen, and even leg muscles. The symptoms wax and wane. As Gilles de la Tourette remarked in 1885, this condition presents many obsessions and compulsions; in the United States, however, the illness was always considered to be a neurological condition without major mental components. This might not be so. In 1975 we began to emphasize the presence of obsessions and compulsions, as well as family disturbance. We believe this disorder affects the psychological and social makeup of the patient. Nowadays, the mental components of the disorder are widely accepted.

There are also a substantial number of Tourette's patients who self-mutilate. They bite their mouths, nails, cuticles, and hands. They bang their heads, slap their faces, and so forth. The following symptoms are characteristic of Tourette's syndrome:

Blinking	Guttural sounds
Squinting	Sudden cursing (copralalia)
Twitching	Mimicking others' gestures
Frowning	(echokinesis)
Eye rolling	Repeating others' words
Sniffing	(echolalia)
Hissing	Obsessions
Throat clearing	Compulsions
Spitting	Aggression
Hiccuping	Self-mutilation

TREATMENT FOR GILLES DE LA TOURETTE'S SYNDROME

The most popular treatments consist of the use of major tranquilizers, Haldol® (haloperidol) and Orap 24® (pimozide), and anti–obsessive-compulsive agents. The advantage of giving anti–obsessive-compulsive drugs alone, or in combination with Haldol or Orap 24, is that the obsessive-compulsive symptoms are also controlled.

Psychological and family therapy intervention is a crucial aspect of treatment. The family constellation disturbance very much affects the treatment outcome. Family members of patients suffering from Tourette's may have related psychiatric disorders suggesting a genetic link. As with OCD, Tourette's syndrome is a chronic condition. The aim of therapy is to help the patient to function in the best possible way.

John is a thirty-eight-year-old executive and a Wall Street success who has come a long way from the child who spat, blinked, twitched, contorted, and produced funny noises. He was the school scapegoat, scorned and rejected by his peer group and, unfortunately, misunderstood by his teachers. John's concerned parents took him to his pediatrician, who reassured them by saying, "John has childhood tics that will disappear in time." This was not the case.

At the age of twelve John was diagnosed as having Gilles de la Tourette's syndrome. His psychiatrist put him on Haldol, and his symptoms improved within two weeks. Unfortunately, he developed neurological side effects consisting of mouth movements and tremors. Medication was changed to other major tranquilizers. When he was referred to us we tried him on a combination of L-Tryptophan and an anti–obsessive-compulsive drug, which became the treatment of choice. We saw partial improvement.

I will lose my freedom, yet I'm so dependent on others!

My obsessive thoughts are like an old scratched record. It keeps repeating itself. It won't stop.

My obsessions are unacceptable, unwelcomed guests.

According to the police records, I didn't hit a car or injure anyone. But you know how it is, police are overworked. I will keep double-checking.

5

A Bird's-eye View

The Integral Approach to Treatment

Traditionally, psychiatric treatment consists of biological, psychological, social, and combined approaches. These therapies are directed to achieve specific goals such as symptom suppression, symptom improvement, and general goals for rehabilitation and social readjustment. Furthermore, therapy should target improvements in family interaction and the patient's working ability.

Unfortunately, very often the mode of therapy used is determined by the therapist's orientation rather than by the treatment's curative properties. Unknowingly, a patient who consults a psychologist may be treated only with psychological techniques. Contrarily, a patient consulting a psychiatrist might be treated mainly with medication. If we consider a patient to be an integral being, however, then the body, the emotions, and the intellect should be treated at the same time, with the participation of the family. The patient's environment should also be considered. Social illnesses, such as venereal disease or those caused by ecological contamination, may also affect a person's behavior. Looking at a disease as the loss of equilibrium, existing within and without ourselves, we can understand the importance of an integral approach to the treatment of any illness, including OCD.

Let us, for example, look at a patient who has a fear of germs. This patient is afraid that germs existing in the water may contaminate him and eventually cause his death. The patient keeps sending water samples for analysis, even when he is told that the water is pure and okay to drink. That's not enough; he's still afraid. One day, the water actually does become contaminated by local industry. Consequently, the patient's symptoms are reinforced, and he worsens. A good example of irrational response to social illness is AIDS. In the case of phobic patients, the fear of getting AIDS has assumed gigantic proportions.

THE EFFECT ON THE FAMILY

The family binds us together in a set of values and beliefs. The family provides nourishment, housing, education, love, and care. At least this is what we expect, or what we believe a family should be. Sometimes an emotional disorder present in one or more members of the family breaks the bond of the family. On other occasions, the opposite occurs, and a disease may bring the family together. But a mental illness eventually erodes the foundation of the family. Emotional disorders bring with them misunderstanding, moodiness, distrust, anger, and excessive demands. A nonfunctional patient, continuously obsessing, or a patient with a compulsion demanding family members to join him or her in the performance of rituals (such as handwashing, double-checking, and so forth) may produce family disturbance. In addition, if a patient is economically dependent on the family, there is further stress on the family, which may lead to resentment, anger, and similar emotions.

We would like to emphasize that emotional and physical surroundings have an influence on the patient's illness. The ideal program should include simultaneous treatment for the individual, the family, and the social environment where the individual dwells. Since achieving this is highly improbable, we deal with the patient during the acute phase of the illness, and we limit ourselves to teaching the family how to handle the patient's needs.

TREATMENT FOR OCD

OCD treatment consists of medication or psychological therapies, or a combination of these. Much less used forms of therapy consist of psychosurgery and sleep therapy or such nontraditional therapies as special diets, vitamins, physical exercise, meditation, and yoga.

Are these therapies useful to treat OCD? Some therapies are considered the treatment of choice, although other therapies may be indicated for a specific patient.

Am I one of thousands of patients with OCD who will receive the same treatment approach? Although you are one out of thousands of patients, you are an individual with unique characteristics, and therefore your treatment should be tailored to fit your needs.

What are the goals of therapy? Our goals for therapy are to

suppress symptoms

relieve the intensity of symptoms

reduce the frequency of symptoms

reduce the duration of symptoms

rehabilitate

improve social adjustment

develop working skills

restore working ability

improve family relations

improve social relations

Who should choose my therapy? Only a qualified professional should choose your treatment — of course, with your approval.

How does a therapist choose my treatment? In general, a psychologist will choose psychotherapy while a psychiatrist will be inclined to select drug therapy. Since OCD has both medical and psychological aspects, a combined treatment is best.

The Integral Approach to OCD Treatment

A human being is an individual system made up of the sum of the body, the intellect, and the emotions. Since we live within a family and a social system, all these systems must interact to obtain a harmonious balance. Coexistence may be peaceful or diseased. When a disease strikes at any of the systems, all the other systems are affected. All these systems work like a machine and will need to be lubricated.

In what way will these systems affect me? A patient suffering from OCD may show impairment in any or all of the following areas: physical well-being, emotions, intellectual capacity, and family and social relations.

Good treatment must consider all these factors to restore health and put the system back into operation. This treatment modality is known as the *integral approach.*

General Concepts of Treatment

Therapy should suppress or decrease the intensity of symptoms. The idea is to control your illness, rather than allowing the illness to control you. OCD control imposes a daily task of perseverance and patience. Because of the severity of OCD symptoms, patients will be very anxious and depressed. Therefore, the tendency is to first treat the existing anxiety and/or depression, rather than the symptoms of obsessions and compulsions. To treat OCD, we favor an all-around program based on an integrative approach. The program may include behavioral and cognitive therapy, psychopharmacotherapy, family therapy, and rehabilitation.

What kind of therapy is going to be used? When will it be used? To answer these questions, the following steps must be taken:

1. obtain a diagnosis in order to classify the type of obsessive-compulsive disorder
2. have a solid idea of the duration, intensity, and frequency of symptoms
3. evaluate the degree of severity
4. determine the gap between onset of illness and time of first consultation
5. be acquainted with the various forms of treatment
6. know the treatment outcome

7. have all laboratory test results available
8. have the results of psychological tests

Having these elements, we should be able to determine the mode of treatment and discuss treatment alternatives as well. In order to obtain a good treatment outcome, therapy must have enough time to work, so improvement can be demonstrated. There are no miracle cures, and recovery comes only gradually. Remember, too, that many OCD patients come for therapy only after years of illness.

PATIENTS WHO DO NOT IMPROVE

Several explanations can be offered for patients who do not improve. For example, if a patient is misdiagnosed, treatment is destined to fail. If OCD becomes a way of life, then the patient simply cannot give up the symptoms. Sometimes, the patient can use his or her illness to advantage, and in other cases, the family gains an advantage. Other reasons for lack of improvement are discussed in detail in other parts of this book.

We have to tailor the right treatment to the right patient. We must treat a patient who has an illness and not a disease present in the patient. For instance, patient A, treated with an anti–obsessive-compulsive drug of fifty milligrams three times per day, improves very well. Yet patient B, having the same disease and given the same medication and dosage, may not benefit from the medication. Giving patient B a higher dose of the medication may do wonders, however. Medication titration, or dosage handling, is a key factor in good results.

I take medication, but I don't improve. Sometimes medication dosage is appropriate, but the patient does not improve. What can be done? First, we look into the duration of treatment. The administration of tricyclic antidepressants for OCD usually requires three to four weeks before showing improvement. Second, there are minimum drug blood levels needed to have a therapeutic effect. Contrarily, excessive drug blood levels may have a negative effect. This is known as the *therapeutic window*—the range in which the medication works best. Therefore, if poor results are obtained, the therapeutic window may help to determine whether or not the drug is efficacious. Third, the patient may be skipping medication. He or she may believe the drugs are not helpful and won't bother taking them. Fourth, the patient may be drinking alcohol or using cocaine, marijuana, or other substances that might interfere with the action of the medication. Fifth, the medication alone is not enough. A patient may require additional treatment, such as behavioral therapy. Sixth, a patient may find it advantageous to remain ill (for example, to remain dependent, to avoid responsibility, or to receive economic benefits). Seventh, one or more family members may benefit from keeping the patient ill (for instance, distracting one from other problems, keeping a marriage together by having a common cause, or satisfying a need to be a martyr).

The Biological Basis of OCD

The brain functions by activating a network of cells. All these messages come and go using nerve bundles (nervous highways) and chemical bridges. These bridges are chemical substances known as neurotransmitters. The best known neurotransmitters are epinephrine, norepinephrine, serotonin, dopamine, and acetylcholine. These neurotransmitters participate in the regulation of our emotions. They have been associated with schizophrenia, depression, anxiety, and obsessive-compulsive disorder. Of all of them, serotonin seems to be the one most closely associated with OCD. This conclusion is the result of two findings: some drugs raising serotonin levels appear to be effective in the treatment of OCD; in some patients, serotonin levels have been decreased or altered.

Research done in the area of brain activity has indicated that both frontal lobes and the basal ganglia (a cerebral region associated with Parkinson's disease) might be affected in OCD.

Position emission tomography (PET), a technique applied to study the metabolism of the brain, has shown that sugar metabolism is abnormal in the brains of patients with OCD. Electroencephalogram (brain-wave tracing) has been found to be abnormal in a group of obsessive-compulsive patients. One special brain-wave tracing technique has shown there are frontal lobe abnormalities in OCD. Finally, neuropsychological testing has detected organic deficit in the brains of some patients with OCD.

Research to detect the biological basis of OCD is still continuing. There is no conclusive evidence that OCD is strictly an organic illness. Yet we now have information indicating that some patients suffering from OCD belong to the biological category of OCD.

In what way will this knowledge help me? The more you know about OCD, the better understanding you will have of it. Consequently, better treatment can be offered. Research projects, by fostering knowledge, may help to close existing gaps in the understanding of OCD. What we know today about the biology of OCD has helped to close many gaps. When hope dims, new advancements tells us to keep hanging on and never give up.

My brother lived 350 miles away from me, but I called him every night to be sure that he had checked out the gas jets. Once he had done so, I was able to fall asleep. Later, I asked him to start checking for closed doors, lights, and windows too. He became quite upset, and now he has an unlisted phone number.

You are right, doctor. I can ask the same questions under different disguises. I also have a list of people whom I ask the same question. I do it for two reasons—one, to keep them from thinking I am stupid, ignorant, unable to comprehend their answers, and second, because I can double-check them as well.

I only use two bars of soap a day to take baths and wash my hands. The problem is that my husband is filthy.

As a joke, they gave me a magnifier for Christmas. But I couldn't care less. Now I am capable of detecting every fingerprint left on my furniture. I am proud of a really clean house.

Look, here are the pictures of myself looking at the mirror. Now I know it is me. But tomorrow—who knows?

6

The Behavioral Approach

B EHAVIOR therapy emphasizes the importance of learning habits. It offers a learning theory to explain how fears and compulsions are acquired and how they are later maintained. While it does not deny the existence of a biological or possible genetic basis, it does not deal with it.

The first part of the learning theory is known as *classical conditioning* and the second part as *operant conditioning*. You may have heard of Pavlov's dog, which learned to salivate to the sound of a bell. This was the beginning of classical conditioning. If this type of learning is applied to OCD, then we can say that somehow a neutral object (such as a doorknob with a red spot) becomes associated in the mind of the patient with an innate fear (such as dying or becoming ill). The patient thinks the red spot is likely to be AIDS-contaminated blood, and therefore she may die. Of course, the possibility of death or illness produces a lot of anxiety. Slowly the doorknob becomes paired with different objects, places, and the like. Eventually, everything becomes connected to the doorknob, which ultimately elicits anxiety on its own. It is with classical conditioning that the fears are learned and with operant conditioning, the second part of the learning theory, that they are maintained. During operant conditioning, patients learn new behaviors (compulsions) that decrease their anxiety when confronted with feared objects or places. Thus patients' compulsive behavior becomes reinforced because it reduces anxiety or discomfort.

Sometimes the fear disappears, but the compulsions remain. What function does the compulsion serve if not to reduce anxiety? Sometimes compulsions continue to be reinforcing because they avert possible harm and provide a sense of safety. For example, patients who keep checking the doors at night may not experience fear, but the double-checking makes them feel safe. Although compulsions themselves may produce a lot of anxiety (because of the time and energy needed to perform them), they are maintained because the rewarding, or anxiety-reducing, effects are greater than the punitive aspects.

Behavior therapy does not offer a good explanation for the acquisition and maintenance of obsessions. Several hypotheses have been offered, but none seems very convincing. One theory is that obsessions come in two stages. First they are aversive and second, anxiety-reducing. It is the discomfort-reducing aspect that maintains the obsession. Another theory is that patients with obsessions are highly intelligent and have probably been rewarded socially and economically for thinking. Unlike others, they may be less likely to put aside uncomfortable thoughts because they believe everything is solvable. This second explanation may be true about people who have obsessive-compulsive traits, but this is not our experience with obsessional patients. In fact, they are usually unable to solve problems and are dependent upon others to do it for them. A third explanation is that morbid obsessions reduce aggression, especially if the individual is nonassertive. We feel behavioral therapy inadequately explains the presence of obsessions. This doesn't mean that behavioral treatment is ineffective, however. In fact, for some types of obsessions, behavior therapy may be quite useful.

What treatments are available? While many treatments are offered, they are not necessarily the right ones for OCD. Some forms of drug and behavior therapy are the most widely researched and accepted and appear to yield the best results. But be cautious in choosing the right form of treatment. Don't take for granted that the proper treatment will be administered. Be sure to ask the right questions. In order to do so, you must be thoroughly acquainted with the treatment approaches. Let's start with behavior therapy.

What can I expect from behavior therapy? Behavior therapy is a general term to describe a variety of treatment techniques that are tested and found to change undesirable behaviors. Not all forms of behavior therapy are appropriate in the treatment of OCD. In fact, the only one found effective is exposure and response prevention and, to some extent, cognitive therapy used in conjunction with it. Cognitive therapy tries to change patients' illogical or faulty beliefs about their fears by challenging their beliefs. (We will discuss cognitive therapy later in this chapter.) A common term used to describe exposure and response prevention is *flooding,* which means to have patients experience tremendous anxiety by facing their fears. This type of treatment is modified to meet the patient's needs. A thorough analysis of the problem and information about the whole patient is necessary before treatment begins.

Georgia, who suffered from OCD for ten years, had tried all types of therapy, but to no avail. We offered some anti–obsessive-compulsive drugs and behavior therapy. She told us she had already had behavior therapy and it hadn't helped her. We questioned her further about what actually took place in the behavioral sessions. She described relaxation exercises and being taken out of the office three or four times and asked to touch things. We told her this was not the type of behavior therapy we prescribe for a condition like hers. At the time of the interview, Georgia was washing her hands twenty times a day, ten times up to the elbow.

Her problems began when she left home to go to college. At first she found herself chasing classmates all over the campus to return pens and notebooks she had taken by mistake. She couldn't wait until the next day; they might need the objects that night. Then she started repeatedly asking others if they understood what she said. Just in case, she would phrase things a million different ways to make sure she was not misunderstood. Georgia thought these behaviors were bizarre, but it was not until she felt contaminated and began to wash that she became very upset.

One day in her chemistry laboratory she noticed a sign on a gas jet that read "Beware, Poisonous Gas." All the other students went right past the gas jet, leaned against it, touched it, and went about their business. Not Georgia. She developed an urge to wash her hands because her sleeve touched it accidentally. She washed and thought that was the end of it. But slowly she found that she couldn't get close to the sign without washing. Eventually, she withdrew from chemistry class and thought she would change her major from chemistry. Nonetheless, she found herself washing every time she passed or touched anything or anyone who might have been in the chemistry lab.

Soon she had to travel off-campus to buy soap and shampoo. She dropped her meal plan and starved most of the time because the student cashier was also a chemistry major. When her roommates slept, she showered for several hours. Georgia was also afraid of being poisoned and at times poisoning others. She wanted to tell everyone about the dangers of eating in the school cafeteria but knew her fears were ridiculous. Georgia was bright and determined to finish school, and she did. Her family was aware she was having problems and sent her to various psychiatrists and psychologists. By the time she came to us, she was afraid of grocery stores in her hometown and her kitchen because she thought the cleaning items were all poisonous.

Our treatment program consisted of daily ninety-minute sessions for several weeks, gradually cutting back to one session a week. For the first several weeks, we allowed a monitored ten-minute shower every fifth day. We exposed Georgia gradually to various appliances in her kitchen, while telling her that she and her family would be poisoned by the cleaning agent that had touched the countertop. We asked her to touch cleaning items, bug sprays, fertilizers, plant food, and the like. We then visited supermarkets, local universities, and hospitals. Georgia was taught to flood herself, in other words to expose herself to everything she senselessly feared and to verbalize her fears as if they were going to occur.

She soon began going places, touching "poisonous" items, and verbalizing to herself that she and all the other thousands of people who had touched that particular item would soon die. In the process, if they touched others, they too would die, and so on. Within six months to one year Georgia no longer experienced an urge to wash. We began to work on her dependency and nonassertiveness problems, as well as her fears of being alone.

With exposure and response prevention, first the intensity, next the duration, and finally the frequency of thoughts about the fear decrease. In judging improvement, it is important to pay attention to all three and not to feel discouraged if all these aspects do not change simultaneously.

Larry was a collector, and so were his parents, but they didn't know it. Larry's behavior stood out in this family of collectors because his bed nearly touched the ceiling, and he had to climb a ladder to get into bed. His pockets were filled with wrappers, and he retained a file on every aspect of computers. He was thirty years old, living at home, and worked as a train conductor. He had a personal computer at home that he used occasionally, but he had no desire to study computers at the time. His parents saved odds and ends and also had a file on newspaper clippings of interest for the previous twenty years.

If Larry had not had a problem with his bed, he may not have come for treatment at this point. The difference between his parents and himself was that they didn't experience the same degree of anxiety over throwing things out, and their behavior remained limited to certain items. Perhaps they all were eccentric, yet Larry developed OCD. Larry feared disaster if he discarded items that he might need sometime. He worried that he'd never again have access to something that might be important. He knew his fears were unreasonable, and he knew that he never looked at his collections.

We went to Larry's house and helped him gradually throw out everything. In addition, we had him purchase things, use them immediately, and throw them out. We challenged his beliefs about discarding important items and needing them later on. We encouraged him to flood himself. He would throw out a candy wrapper and tell himself that his train ticket might have been stuck to it. Consequently, he would be late for work the next day and get in trouble.

While throwing out his file on computers he would tell himself that he would never be able to study computers or purchase the right one because he would not have access to the information if he needed it. Larry's treatment continued until his bed rested on the floor and he no longer collected things.

We were concerned that he might return to the old habits, because his parents were less inclined to reinforce "noncollecting behavior." They didn't see anything wrong with it, as long as it was limited. They had difficulty understanding that Larry, in the long run, would probably not be able to limit his collecting compul-

sion. We referred the three of them to group family therapy and
Larry to a self-help group.

Mary had been unable to leave her house for the last four years.
Before then she was able to go to the supermarket a couple of
blocks away and just prior to that, back and forth to work, five
miles away. At the time of the consultation, her parents were
bringing her food and other necessities. Professionals who had
seen or spoken to her by phone diagnosed her as agoraphobic
because she became anxious whenever she left her secure environment. She had gradually become housebound; she was not
agoraphobic, however, and you shall see why.

When we visited her home and questioned her in detail, it
became apparent that she would get anxious upon leaving the
house, fearing something terrible would happen. She spent hours
checking that the stove, oven, appliances, light switches, and
faucets were all turned off, and all doors were shut. She also had
to make sure that the bed was made, everything was organized,
the toilet was flushed, and her lingerie and sexual paraphernalia
were hidden.

At first when she was able to work, her checking compulsion
did not take much time, and she believed that if anything happened she could return home immediately. She had informed her
neighbors to call her if a fire or robbery occurred. As the symptoms progressed, she became less and less certain that her neighbors would be around to inform her, that she might not be reach-
able immediately, and by the time she arrived home, the fire
fighters or police officers would have gone through her belongings. She also believed that she would be held responsible for the
fire or robbery and that her neighbors would be critical of her.

She quit her job, went on disability, and allowed herself to
leave the house for short periods of time to purchase necessities.
Gradually, as her anxiety increased, she could not even do that
and became totally housebound. Agoraphobia was a misdiag-
nosis, however, because she didn't fear the physical symptoms
that occurred when she was anxious; instead she feared the pre-
sumed disastrous consequences of not double-checking.

During her exposure and response prevention treatment, we
directed her to plug in her appliances, leave light switches on, let

the water run slightly, and not make her bed. We told her that a fire or robbery would occur, and the whole town would know her private life and talk about her at dinner every night. They would criticize her for being careless, a loose woman, disorganized, undesirable, and so forth. This approach continued until she accepted her beliefs as unreasonable. We also used cognitive therapy to challenge her belief that she needed everyone's approval and that she couldn't withstand criticism.

Gradually, we increased the distance from Mary's home while exposing her to her fears. We recommended family therapy to her parents to learn how to stop enabling her, or unconsciously encouraging her compulsions. In family therapy, Mary's parents learned not to feel guilty for not buying groceries or taking care of her other needs. Mary was able to resume work, and in follow-up sessions we worked on developing a social network, which included dating and increasing her self-esteem.

The S. family is a good illustration of the pervasiveness of a compulsion. Mr. S. worked as an executive in a large corporation. He believed that his coworker Rob looked sick and was dying of AIDS. Thus he avoided any contact with Rob. He washed his hands every time he touched a paper Rob had touched, and then he began to wash every time he thought Rob might have used the photocopy machine, sat on a chair, or leaned against a desk. Since he worked in Manhattan, where he thought the incidence of AIDS was the greatest, he was convinced that certain sick-looking people were dying of AIDS.

When he arrived at his suburban home, he would immediately go to the basement, take off his clothes, and carefully put them into a bag that was to be taken to the dry cleaners the next day. He built himself a shower in the basement, and he would wash and decontaminate himself before seeing his family. He would run upstairs naked to put on "clean" clothes. These clothes could not be brought downstairs, since that was the contaminated area, and no one or nothing "clean" was allowed there. The children would have to remain in their rooms while he ran upstairs this way. They were never permitted to touch or have any contact with their father before he showered. If by accident he touched or thought his clothes touched a toy outside or the staircase railings, he insisted they be sterilized or discarded. A bicycle, a toy car, balls, and many children's toys had been thrown out. Every day Mrs. S. would decontaminate the front doorknob and the lock with bleach.

Gradually, Mr. S. avoided his children if they had cuts, even if he had showered. He wanted to be 100 percent sure the children would not get AIDS. His children were told not to kiss him hello or good-bye or touch him until he had thoroughly inspected them for cuts. Mrs. S. was always using bleach, which Mr. S. was convinced would kill the AIDS virus. Of course, Mr. S. had had doubts about the validity of his beliefs. He sometimes found them ridiculous, but he couldn't help himself. Mrs. S., who cooperated initially, decided she had had enough of this "nonsense" and would no longer use bleach or throw out toys. This caused her husband to verbally and physically abuse her, and she soon went back to washing and decontaminating things for him. Clearly, the marriage was on the rocks, and she was concerned about the effect the bizarre behavior was having on the children.

After watching a television program on OCD, Mrs. S. identified the symptoms and eventually brought her husband to us for treatment. Mrs. S. was considering divorce. We asked her to delay her decision until Mr. S. received treatment. She was extremely angry and did not wish to cooperate in his therapy. We enlisted her help by telling her that she would no longer need to perform his compulsions for him.

Very slowly we exposed Mr. S. to items, places, and people he thought were possible contaminants. We didn't allow him to shower or to change his clothes for several days at a time. He wasn't permitted to send his clothes to the dry cleaners or to use disinfectants. He had to take a leave of absence from work while he underwent treatment. He was given an anti–obsessive-compulsive medication to enable him to go through behavior therapy.

Although Mr. S. improved and resumed work, Mrs. S. was still angry. Her feelings for her husband hadn't changed. They were referred to marital therapy, and the children were asked to come for several sessions to assess if they had acquired any symptoms or if they had questions about their family situation. The family had been destroyed, and Mrs. S. believed she could no longer live with her husband. They divorced.

While in individual therapy, Mr. S. continued to improve as he dealt with the guilt of what had happened to his family. He believed that his symptoms had been noticed at work and that his promotion was in jeopardy because he took a leave of absence. He worried excessively over losing his job and ending up in the Bowery. With cognitive therapy, we helped challenge these beliefs. Eventually, he got another job because he couldn't face his coworkers who had been aware of his strange behaviors. His relationship with his children improved, and he started a new life with a new wife.

All the above cases illustrate how behavior therapy is used with primarily compulsive patients. A similar approach may be used with patients who are more obsessional, as in the following case.

Mr. F. was a happily married father of two. He was disturbed by several obsessions. He spent hours obsessing about a parking ticket he received five years previously when he mistakenly parked his car in a reserved parking lot of the county court. He was a decent man, yet he experienced morbid obsessions of stabbing or choking his wife, and he also had sexual thoughts about his children. These thoughts would come to mind spontaneously, and no matter how he tried to avoid them, they remained. He was embarrassed and yet afraid that he would act on these impulsive obsessions.

We exposed Mr. F. to his thoughts and had him think about them in minute detail. We taped the flooding sessions and had him listen to them at home. We asked him to get close to his wife while holding sharp objects. When he felt ready to share some of his obsessions with his wife, we explained to her that these thoughts were not disguised angry feelings toward her and that he was not a child molester. We indicated that these were common obsessions and she had nothing to fear. Obsessional patients do not act out their impulsive thoughts.

When she felt more comfortable, we had Mr. F. put his hands around his wife's neck to prove to himself that he would never act out his fears. The same method of flooding in imagination was used with his obsession about the parking ticket. At first his anxiety about the obsessions decreased, then he noticed a change in the duration. The thoughts still came to mind, although for only a few seconds each time. At that time we recommended medication that helped decrease the frequency of his obsessions. Sometimes anti – obsessive-compulsive drugs are as good as or better than behavior therapy for obsessional patients. This combination may still be the best approach.

How does behavior therapy work? By continuously exposing patients to their fears and preventing them from engaging in their obsessions and compulsions, *habituation* occurs. Habituation is the process by which we reduce patients' fearful responses by getting them used to stimuli. Consequently, patients will not feel as anxious about their obsessions or their fears. They learn that their fears will not be realized, and they begin to think differently.

Many psychophysiological studies have proved that habituation lessens fears. These studies measure heart rate, respiration frequency, and skin temperature. Researchers have found that initially all these physiological responses increase with exposure and then decrease (habituate). In other words, patients first show all the physiological reactions of fear, such as increased heart rate, increased respiration frequency, and lower skin temperature. Then, after continued exposure to their fears, the fear disappears.

Is cognitive therapy helpful? We all know that some people make the best of most situations, and others seem to be miserable no matter what happens. This attitude toward life may be determined by our genes, by our early childhood training, and by the way we talk to ourselves. To some extent, we have the capacity to change the way we think and thereby the way we feel.

Think back to a time when you said something nasty to a loved one, such as "I think you should learn how to dress better." Remember how you were influenced, not only by your actions and their consequences, but by the thoughts, images, and feelings before, during, and after the incident. Your feelings resulted from your thoughts: he will hate me, he will think badly of me, he will reject me. You probably were tense, nervous, and fearful anticipating his negative reaction or outburst. You felt this way because of what you were saying to yourself.

Cognitive therapy is a form of behavioral treatment that teaches people to change their thoughts, and thereby their feelings in a given situation. There are many types of cognitive therapy: self-instructional training; self-dialogue; cognitive restructuring; and stress inoculation training.

Self-instructional training refers to learning to think certain thoughts before acting. For example, if you say, "I will succeed in learning how to drive a stick shift," you are more likely to succeed than if you say, "I will never learn; I am a clumsy person."

Self-dialogue refers to our internal debates about what we should do. All of us weigh alternatives before making decisions, no matter how trivial. Think back to the last time you bought a pair of pants to wear to a party. You compared the various styles, colors, and prices before settling on the pair you wanted. During this form of therapy, patients are taught how to solve problems and talk to themselves positively and logically in order to feel better.

For example, if while choosing pants you think, "Everybody at the party will think I am an idiot if I wear these pants," you are likely not to buy them even if you like them. Therefore, it is better to say, "It doesn't matter what others think; I'm going to buy them because I like them."

Rational-emotive therapy (RET) is one form of cognitive restructuring therapy that we use most often with OCD patients. Cognitive restructuring techniques modify patients' thinking and challenge the premises, assumptions, and attitudes underlying their beliefs. The basic premise of rational-emotive therapy is that much emotional suffering is owing to the irrational ways people think about the world and the assumptions they make. Several examples of RET will be given later on.

Stress inoculation training involves teaching patients to identify their stressful reactions and to learn how to practice copying skills—first in imagination, then in reality. A variety of therapeutic techniques are used to teach coping skills, such as positive thinking, problem solving, dialoguing with oneself, and rewarding oneself for coping well.

These cognitive therapies have been researched and found to be effective in the treatment of depression, but they have not been well tested in the treatment of OCD. Cognitive therapy, which primarily challenges the OCD patient's irrational fears, may have been haphazardly used during exposure and response prevention, but the latter was always the primary focus of treatment. Therapists believed that cognitive changes were to occur spontaneously as a result of flooding. In other words, patients would start to think more logically and spontaneously during the course of treatment; their thoughts would contradict the irrational beliefs that had formed the basis of their fears. Until recently, however, cognitive therapy was used neither alone nor in conjunction with exposure and response prevention in any systematic way. We think there *cannot* be a lasting change in OCD symptoms unless the patient learns to think indifferently; therefore we believe cognitive therapy is the tool to correct the beliefs. Cognitive therapy should be used together with exposure and response prevention and not as a substitute for it, although some preliminary studies of ours demonstrate RET alone to be effective in the treatment of pure obsessions. Another area where cognitive therapy shows promise is with patients who have *overvalue ideation* (strong belief in their fears). Again, we first use the cognitive approach to lessen patients' belief in their fears.

Patients overestimate the possibility of the occurrence of their fears. For example, a patient with OCD is likely to believe that the chance of getting AIDS during a routine blood drawing is 80 percent, while most people estimate zero to 1 percent. In addition, patients with OCD tend to underestimate their ability to cope with disastrous consequences. We have identified some of the most common faulty beliefs in the OCD patient to be the following:

I must have guarantees

I cannot stand the anxiety/discomfort

I must not make mistakes

I am responsible for causing harm

I am responsible for not preventing harm to others

Thinking is the same as acting

It is awful, horrible, terrible to make the wrong decision

There is a right and a wrong in every situation

I must have complete control over everything at all times

I am in continuous danger

I am responsible for others

I must be perfect

Jane was a divorced mother of two who worked as a second-grade teacher. She would spend hours at night preparing lessons for the next day. She would obsess over her students' problems, such as whether a child in her classroom could be referred to the school psychologist to be tested for a learning disability. She believed that if she made any wrong decision, her students' lives would be destroyed. If she didn't teach everything she thought should be taught in the second grade, she would be responsible for the students' failure in later grades or possibly in life. Jane believed she was solely responsible for each student's development.

Because she felt this way, Jane had no time for leisure activities. She stayed late after school, talking to the students, preparing her lessons, and then going over her own children's homework repeatedly. On weekends, her mother would care for her two children while she prepared lesson plans for the students or made up new bulletin boards. At night, she would spend some time with her children and go to bed early, exhausted. Jane eventually became depressed. She had no pleasure in her life, only work.

We treated her by using cognitive therapy. We attacked her faulty thoughts, such as there was only one right decision; that she was solely responsible for her students; that she must never make mistakes; and that she be perfect. As she changed her beliefs, her obsession and depression lifted, and she found more time to have fun. Changing one's beliefs is a long, hard process that must be worked on continuously.

Will my treatment be different if I am obsessional rather than compulsive? Most compulsive patients are obsessional as well, although their obsessions are usually related to their compulsions. Not all obsessional patients are compulsive, however. Some patients have pure obsessions with neither motor nor mental compulsion. Mental compulsions refer to the performance of certain rituals or sayings in one's mind in order to prevent some feared catastrophe. For example, Don couldn't walk into another room or pick up an object if a bad thought came to mind. He would force himself to think about a "good" word or a pleasant experience before going on with his activity. Other mental compulsions consist of activities such as counting a certain number of times to procure something desired, imagining a geometric design, and/or praying repeatedly to counteract an unacceptable thought. Motor compulsions, which we've discussed previously, include handwashing, double-checking, collecting, and the like.

We believe that for those patients who have pure obsessions, the nature of those obsessions is important in predicting treatment outcome. Morbid or impulsive obsessions, such as fear regarding the committing of an aggressive, sexual, or religious transgression, are the easiest to treat behaviorally and have the best prognosis. Obsessions that have disastrous consequences, such as becoming ill, dying, or making a fool of oneself also respond well to current treatment.

Ellen was obsessed with the number thirteen, with hurting her children, with thinking of a "good" word before picking up an object, and with the undoing in her head of a superstitious thought. All of these obsessions had a disastrous consequence attached to them. Numbers that added up to thirteen, the thirteenth page in a magazine, and channel thirteen on television all had to be avoided whenever possible, or her mother was going to die. Of course, it was not always possible to avoid such things. At other times she would experience morbid (impulsive) obsessions of throwing her children down the stairs. What had started out as "a head game" (her terminology) became an incapacitating obsession. She would tell herself that if a "good" thought popped into her head, she could pick up a pen or the telephone or answer the doorbell and good things would happen. Then she thought she'd better undo a "bad" word by avoiding an object until a "good" word came to her. Before long, only bad words were popping into her mind and she was becoming catatonic — unable to move, walk in and out of rooms, or pick up objects.

Ellen's obsessions were treated by anti–obsessive-compulsive medication and behavior therapy. The latter is more effective for

Ellen's type of obsession, in which there is a theme, an undoing or neutralizing act, or a disastrous consequence. In Ellen's case, we exposed her to the number thirteen and had her think about her mother dying. We cajoled her into doing things while she thought of "bad" words. Her behavior therapy sessions took place in various locations; sometimes she listened to audiotapes about her fears. She did quite well with this treatment.

The most difficult obsessions to treat are those that don't have a theme. They consist of isolated thoughts with no meaning attached to them, such as a line from a song, a melody, counting numbers, an isolated sentence, review of conversations, or images of objects and people.

Another difficult obsession to treat is characterized by doubting and indecisiveness. Patients with this type of obsession tend to overanalyze, be tangential and circumstantial, and continually try to solve unsolvable problems. It is frustrating for family members, friends, and even the therapist to communicate with such patients. Although the therapist may believe he or she has penetrated the obsession and can logically discuss a concern, the patient says, "Yes, but what if . . . ," and the vicious cycle begins again.

Jim was a bright fifty-year-old accountant who was obsessed about the decisions he was making at the firm. He would present a single problem, for example, "Should I have gone to my supervisor and requested a different form than the one I used to send my accounting figures to company ABC?"

We would start asking logical questions: "Is there a specific form for sending that type of information? What would happen if the wrong form were sent? Why did you choose not to go to your supervisor?" Jim would begin answering the questions logically but digress, describing in detail who worked in the firm, what they did, how well they performed their jobs, how long it took them to do the job as compared to himself, all the available forms and who used what form, and so forth. We would attempt to refocus him and use cognitive therapy to challenge his faulty belief that he must never make mistakes or that he must be perfect.

At other times we would use *exposure* in imagination, another form of behavior therapy, wherein he would imagine himself making a mistake and then being fired. As he imagined the scene, he would state that he knew he would never be fired and that he didn't want to be perfect. Yet he would feel compelled to repeat his original question, and the cycle repeated. Medication was the treatment of choice.

The best form of treatment for obsessions, and primarily the difficult obsessions, is drug therapy. Behavior therapy is helpful if the obsessions follow a theme. Most of the time, the combination of medication and behavior therapy should be tried.

Additional Therapies

We have spoken about drug, behavior, and cognitive therapy as treatment choices. Once the obsessive-compulsive symptoms have been treated, and sometimes even during treatment, other therapies may be helpful, such as the following:

Family therapy

Support groups

Self-help groups

Social skills training

Assertion training

Perfectionistic groups

Physical exercise

FAMILY THERAPY

We offer information about the disorder to the families of patients, on both an individual and a group therapy basis. We also teach them the techniques necessary to cope with it. The group provides a support system for the families, who can share their experiences with others and help each other during the difficult times of the patient's treatment.

Support Groups and Self-Help Groups

A support group run by a professional and a self-help group run by patients (nontherapeutic in nature) can greatly benefit patients. Within a group setting they learn that they are not alone and that others understand them. After having felt isolated, they find a place to share their experiences. The group provides assistance in many ways, ranging from emotional support to the dissemination of information to the public so that other patients can identify their problems and seek proper treatment.

Social Skills and Assertion Training Groups

Social skills and assertion training groups can help if a patient is deficient in those areas. Patients who demonstrate problems in interpersonal relations, dating, or the workplace may benefit from learning appropriate behaviors. In addition, their anxiety-producing faulty beliefs and feelings of inadequacy could be corrected. Assertion training teaches people to express their emotions appropriately.

Perfectionistic Groups and Physical Exercise

We have offered patients a "perfectionistic group" where they can challenge each other's perfectionistic needs and are given tasks to perform imperfectly. In addition, we often recommend physical exercise to help reduce stress and anxiety.

Other Psychological Therapies

Some patients have asked if they can benefit from psychoanalysis — psychoanalytically oriented psychotherapy — eclectic, gestalt, structural, or strategic family therapy, or hypnosis. We will discuss each one briefly. It is important to know that within psychology, there are many different treatment approaches stemming from different theories about the cause of a particular disorder. While one approach may be appropriate for one problem, it may not be right for another. You must be certain that you are getting the best available treatment for your own problem. Let's review some of the different approaches.

Psychoanalysis. Psychoanalysis, or psychoanalytically oriented psychotherapy, deals with childhood traumas to treat unresolved conflicts.

Eclectic Therapy. Eclectic therapy means that various techniques of treatment are borrowed from different schools of psychology, depending on the patient's problem. Unfortunately, this sometimes results in a hodgepodge of techniques, lacking clear theoretical understanding of the problem.

Gestalt Therapy. Through gestalt therapy the patient experiences emotions at the same intensity level as in the past.

Family Therapy. Structural and strategic family therapy deal with the whole family and seek to define the patient's problem as a result of a troubled family structure. Although there are differences between the two, both are basically a form of family therapy. Our references in this book to family therapy cannot be applied in the same sense as used above. We believe in providing education, guidance, and support for the families of patients, and it is in that sense that we have used the term.

Hypnosis. Hypnosis is a treatment whereby suggestions are offered by the therapist and later by patients themselves. For example, the suggestion may be to stop an urge or obsession. Although it would be nice if it worked, unfortunately there is no evidence that it does.

All the therapies mentioned above are not only ineffective but may also be contraindicated for OCD. For example, psychoanalytically oriented psychotherapy reinforces the very symptoms the OCD patient is trying to get rid of because it encourages overanalysis and thereby instills more doubts. We therefore advise patients to research their disorders and to educate themselves, rather than rely solely on what mental health professionals tell them.

As a final note, it is important to remember that the current state of the art indicates that treatments of choice include certain drugs; behavior therapy in the form of exposure and response prevention; cognitive therapy in conjunction with it; and in a few cases, psychosurgery. There is no evidence, despite the claim of any therapist, that any other form of treatment is effective. Of course, other forms of treatment may be helpful in dealing with a host of other problems unrelated to OCD.

I cannot be interrupted in the middle of a task. If someone interrupts me, I become really upset.

In order to know that I am seated, I stand up; then I sit to know that I better stand up, just in case I am not seated but standing up.

My obsessions are severe. They never leave me alone. Therefore I designed a technique by which I only think of a dot floating in front of me. I have removed all the furniture but one chair from a room where I sit without thoughts except the dot. From awakening to bedtime it's my dot and I. I can't go on like this forever.

I have been collecting newspapers all my life. You never know when you may use the information. You cannot walk into my house without stepping on newspapers. In fact, they are piled up to the ceiling. My bed is sitting on newspapers. My bed is almost touching the ceiling of my bedroom. To get in bed I use a ladder. I was told by the super my apartment is a fire hazard.

7

The Biological Approach

T HE brain can be treated with medication, as can any other part of the body. Medications used for the brain can modify brain functions, and thereby our emotional output. These drugs are prescribed to reach specific regions of the brain to produce the desired effects. Unfortunately, they are not 100 percent specific. Their action may affect other areas of the brain, sometimes causing side effects. To understand how these drugs work on the obsessive-compulsive disorder, it will help to become acquainted with the brain.

The brain is a living miracle. It is with our brains and our hands that we created the world we live in. Nonetheless, the cerebral cortex, a thin layer of 100 billion brain cells, remains partly unknown to us.

In studies of the human brain, some specific functions have been localized, either by destroying certain parts of the brain with electrical stimulation or through the presence of identifiable diseases that have altered a portion of the brain. The brain has sensory association areas to receive all stimuli coming from outside or inside the body. These areas can pick up sounds, images, temperature changes, touch, and so forth. Other areas of the brain are related to knowledge, storage of memory, processing of thoughts, consciousness, and motor activity. This is important because OCD patients have difficulties with the way their thoughts are processed. Other parts of the brain regulate behavior and response to events that occur outside or inside our bodies. Another region of the brain, the limbic system, controls emotional behavior, as well as body temperature, the drive to eat and drink, body weight, sugar balance, sleep pattern, sexual drive, and anger. All this is important because some of these functions might be affected in OCD.

The brain operates by using electrical and chemical energy. This energy travels across the nerves by using neurotransmitters, chemical bridges that connect one cell to the next. By using these connections, any incoming or outgoing message is carried throughout the nervous system. Finally, in order to function properly, the brain requires good nutrition. The two main nutrients of the brain are oxygen and sugar. Other important nutrients are amino acids, minerals, and vitamins.

Drug Therapy

Pressure, stress, indecisiveness, and uncertainty set the pace of modern life. We live in fear—fear reflected in the tremendous amount of legal and illegal drugs consumed. We spend over $1 billion on tranquilizers for which at least 200 million prescriptions are written each year. This amounts to billions of dollars spent to ease emotional pain or discomfort. As we know it, the brain registers two main types of reactions, pleasure and displeasure. Medication can ease the pain, and certainly OCD is, emotionally, a very painful illness that affects the patient, family, and environment.

In the early 1950s, psychotropic drugs—medicines for the mind—were introduced. Drugs for the brain primarily consist of major tranquilizers, minor tranquilizers, antidepressants, anticonvulsants, and sleeping medication, as shown in table 7 – 1. Use this table to look up any of the medications a patient may have taken or is taking.

Some of these medications have been used to treat OCD. Obsessive-compulsive disorder has been considered a form of anxiety or depression, because both anxiety and depression are very common findings in OCD. That explains the extensive use of anti-anxiety and antidepressant drugs for OCD. In the past, because there were no known anti – obsessive-compulsive medications, physicians resorted to all the other available drugs, hoping to find by trial and error the right drug to treat OCD.

Table 7-1
Alphabetical List of Drug Trade Names, Generic Names, and Drug Types

Trade Name	Generic Name Composition	Drug Type
Akineton	biperiden	anti-Parkinsonian
Amytal	amobarbital	sedative
Anafranil	clomipramine	antidepressant anti–obsessive-compulsive agent
Antabuse	disulfiram	alcohol antagonist
Artane	trihexyphenidyl	anti-Parkinsonian
Atarax	hydroxyzine	anti-anxiety
Aventyl	nortriptyline	antidepressant
Benzedrine	amphetamine	stimulant
Beta-chlor	chloral betaine	sedative
Biphetamine	dextroamphetamine	stimulant
Bromural	bromisovalum	anti-anxiety
Buspar	buspirone	anti-anxiety
Butisol	butabarbital	sedative
Carbrital	pentobarbital carbromal	sedative
Celontin	methsuximide	anticonvulsant
Cogentin	benztropine	anti-Parkinsonian
Compazine	prochlorperazine	anti-anxiety
Cyclazocine	cyclazocine	heroin antagonist
Dalmane	flurazepam	hypnotic
Dartal	thiopropazate	antipsychotic
Deaner	denol	stimulant
Deprol	meprobamate	sedative
Desbutal	methamphetamine	stimulant
Desyrel	trazodone	antidepressant
Dexamyl	dextroamphetamine	stimulant
Dexedrine	dextroamphetamine	stimulant
Dilantin	phenytoin	anticonvulsant
Doriden	glutethimide	hypnotic
Elavil	amitriptyline	antidepressant
Equanil	meprobamate	anti-anxiety
Eskalith	lithium	antimanic
Etrafon	perphenazine amitriptyline	antipsychotic sedative
Eutonyl	pargyline	antidepressant
Felsules	chloral hydrate	sedative
Fluvoxamine	fluvoxamine	antidepressant
Frenquel	azacyclonol	anti-anxiety
Haldol	haloperidol	antipsychotic
Kemadrin	procyclidine	anti-Parkinsonian
Klonopin	clonazepam	anticonvulsant
Lethidrone	nalorphine	heroin substitute
Librium	chlordiazepoxide	anti-anxiety
Lithane	lithium	antimanic
Lithobid	lithium	antimanic

Table 7–1 (continued)

Trade Name	Generic Name Composition	Drug Type
Lithonate	lithium	antimanic
Luminal	phenobarbital	sedative
Marplan	isocarboxazid	antidepressant
Mellaril	thioridazine	antipsychotic
Mesantoin	mephenytoin	anticonvulsant
Miltown	meprobamate	anti-anxiety
Nardil	phenelzine	antidepressant
Navane	thiothixene	antipsychotic
Nembutal	pentobarbital	sedative
Niamid	nialamide	antidepressant
Noctec	chloral hydrate	sedative
Noludar	methyprylon	hypnotic
Norpramin	desipramine	antidepressant
Parnate	tranylcypromine	antidepressant
Permitil	fluphenazine	antipsychotic
Pertofrane	desipramine	antidepressant
Phenergan	promethazine	antipsychotic
Phenobarbital	phenobarbital	sedative
Phenurone	phenacemide	anticonvulsant
Placidyl	ethchlorvynol	hypnotic
Plexonazl	diethylbarbiturate	hypnotic
Preludin	phenmetrazine	stimulant
Proketazine	carphenazine	antipsychotic
Prolixin	fluphenazine	antipsychotic
Prozac	fluoxetine	antidepressant
Ritalin	methylphenidate	stimulant
Seconal	secobarbital	sedative
Serax	oxazepam	anti-anxiety
Serentil	mesoridazine	antipsychotic
Sinequan	doxepin	antidepressant
Sparine	promazine	antipsychotic
Stelazine	trifluoperazine	antipsychotic
Surmontil	trimipramine	antidepressant
Taractan	chlorprothixene	antipsychotic
Tegretol	carbamazepine	antidepressant
Thorazine	chlorpromazine	antipsychotic
Tofranil	imipramine	antidepressant
Triavil	perphenazine	antipsychotic
	amitriptyline	antidepressant
Tri-barbs	secobarbital	sedative
	butabarbital	
	phenobarbital	
Trilafon	perphenazine	antipsychotic
Tybatran	tybamate	anti-anxiety
Valium	diazepam	anti-anxiety
Vistaril	hydroxyzine	anti-anxiety
Vivactil	protriptyline	antidepressant
Wellbutrin	bupropion	antidepressant
Zarontin	ethosuximide	anticonvulsant

TRICYCLIC ANTIDEPRESSANTS

Among the medications used in the past for the treatment of OCD, tricyclic antidepressant drugs appeared to be the best. Tofranil® and Elavil® have been used most frequently, but in the last seventeen years new drugs with more specific anti – obsessive-compulsive action have been discovered. These drugs are classified as antidepressants because they also act on depressive symptoms. There are several promising drugs to treat OCD: Anafranil®, Prozac®, Desyrel®, Fluvoxamine®, and Sertraline®. In addition, L-Tryptophan® (an amino acid), clonidine (an antihypertensive agent), Klonopin® and Dilantin® (anticonvulsant medications), and lithium salts have been tried.

Of all these medications, the most studied and effective treatment appears to be Anafranil (clomipramine). This medication has a favorable treatment outcome in 50 to 70 percent of patients. The possible side effects associated with tricyclic antidepressants are listed in table 7 – 2.

Table 7–2
Common Side Effects of Tricyclic Antidepressants

Medication Side Effects	Cold Turkey Withdrawal Side Effects
Blood pressure changes	Nausea
Fast pulse	Headache
Anxiety	Generalized discomfort
Insomnia	
Tremors	
Dry mouth	
Urinary retention	
Blurred vision	
Constipation	
Skin rash	
Blood count changes	
Nausea	
Diarrhea	
Stomach cramps	
Milk secretion	
Changes in sexual desire	
Weight gain or loss	
Sweating	
Drowsiness	
Fatigue	

NEW DRUGS FOR OCD

Fluoxetine (Prozac) is a bicyclic antidepressant that has recently been made available in the United States for the treatment of depression. We hope it will be approved for the treatment of OCD. One advantage of this drug is that patients usually do not gain weight. A disadvantage is that this drug may increase anxiety. The following are common side effects of Prozac:

Headache	Loss of appetite
Drowsiness	Anxiety
Nausea	Irritability
Abdominal discomfort	Insomnia
Diarrhea	Respiratory infection
Sweating	Allergies

Fluovoxamine (Reid-Rowell), a monocyclic antidepressant, appears promising as an anti – obsessive-compulsive agent. However, it is only available for experimental use. The side effects that are known with this drug are as follows:

Dry mouth	Loss of appetite
Nausea/vomiting	Constipation
Fatigue	Fatigue
Headache	Headache
Pain	Agitation
Blurred vision	Diarrhea

Some other new drugs currently being tested for treatment of OCD are Venlafaxine (Wyeth-Ayerst), Nefazodone (Bristol-Myers), Gepirone (Bristol-Myers), and Sertraline (Pfizer).

MONOAMINE OXIDASE INHIBITORS (MAOIs)

MAOIs have also been used to treat OCD. In the United States, there are two available MAOI drugs: Nardil® and Parnate®. These drugs, while acting differently from the tricyclics, prevent the fast burning of serotonin in the brain. A small number of patients definitely will improve with an MAOI; however, they should be used only when other medications fail. Because of their chemical composition, these drugs may react adversely to certain foods, causing serious side effects as listed below:

Blood pressure changes	Dizziness
Constipation	Dry mouth
Fatigue	Swelling
Stomach upset	Diarrhea
Tremors	Twitching
Anxiety	Hyperactivity
Insomnia	

When taking MAOIs, it is extremely important to report any headaches immediately, and to follow the prescribed diet (see table 7 – 3). Do not take amino acids such as tyrosine, tryptophan, D-L phenylalanine, and phenylalanine. The special diet may hinder long-term compliance with this treatment method and thus hinder success. However, if patients do not adhere to the diet strictly, serious consequences may result.

Lithium Carbonate

Lithium is the treatment of choice for manic-depressive illness. It has also been used for aggressive behavior, depression, schizophrenia, and panic attacks. Our experience has shown that lithium may be effective in patients who have OCD combined with manic illness. There are several reports, including our work, indicating the efficacy of lithium and L-Tryptophan given together for OCD.

L-Tryptophan

L-Tryptophan (TRY) is one of the amino acids present in proteins. This amino acid is essential for the production of serotonin in the body. Because serotonin might be altered in OCD, it has been suggested that TRY might be helpful in improving OCD symptoms. Its administration increases blood serotonin levels.

Table 7-3
Restricted Monoamine Diet for MAOI

Beverages	Dairy	Fish	Meat	Poultry	Vegetables	Other
Wine	Aged cheese	Smoked herring	Brains	Chicken livers	Avocados	Peanut butter
Beer	Sour cream				Tomatoes	Vanilla
Alcohol					Broad beans	Cocoa
Orange juice					Eggplant	Chocolate
Tea[1]						
Coffee[1]						
Soda[2]						

[1] Decaffeinated coffee or tea is allowed.
[2] Without caffeine.

Although TRY is a natural substance, treatment with TRY in large doses must be medically supervised. Because TRY competes with other amino acids for absorption, it should be taken alone and not at the same time as meals containing proteins, such as meat and milk. It might be taken with a carbohydrate meal or, better, with fruit juice. Sugar helps the absorption of TRY in the brain. TRY is better used when taken with niacin (a vitamin of the B complex) and vitamin B-6. In this way TRY becomes available in larger quantities to produce serotonin. Side effects of L-Tryptophan are listed below:

Nausea	Headache
Drowsiness	Excitement
Sleepiness	Aggressive behavior
Paranoid symptoms	Eosinophilia myalgia syndrome

NIACIN

Niacin is one of the vitamins of the B complex. This vitamin is essential to many functions in the nervous system. It is also helpful in lowering cholesterol and fat levels in the blood. Niacin is present in the foods we eat, especially those that contain TRY, because TRY produces both serotonin and niacin. Therefore, if we want to increase serotonin levels, we must saturate the body with niacin in order to force Tryptophan to choose the serotonin pathway. In large doses niacin becomes a drug; as such, it might have side effects, though they are rare. Niacin can cause flushing of the skin. This may be prevented in either of two ways: by taking niacin during a meal on a full stomach or with a glass of milk, or by using a slow-release niacin capsule. Niacin should not be taken if one suffers from peptic ulcer, liver impairment, diabetes, or gout.

VITAMIN B-6

Vitamin B-6 is essential to many functions of the nervous system. It is necessary for the conversion of TRY to serotonin. Therefore, every time TRY is used, vitamin B-6 becomes part of the treatment of OCD. You should know that vitamin B-6 might be depleted by the use of antidepressants, birth control pills, or medication to lower blood pressure. Patients treated with antidepressants, on birth control pills, or on blood-pressure medication should add a small amount of vitamin B-6 to their treatment programs. Large doses of vitamin B-6 may cause neurological problems, but they can be prevented by taking a B-complex tablet.

NUTRITION

Food influences our mood and thinking. We are what we eat. We therefore apply nutritional principles in the treatment of OCD patients. There are diets for heart conditions, liver ailments, kidney dysfunctions, arthritic conditions, and the like. Is there a diet for brain disorders? There is a special diet for the brain when we give MAOI, for certain forms of epilepsy, and for hyperactive behavior. For OCD, there is no specific diet. Some patients with OCD might benefit from a certain diet, however. For example, some OCD patients show an abnormal sugar metabolism. This is tested by performing a five-hour glucose tolerance test. It is known that glucose (sugar) metabolism is closely related to TRY metabolism. TRY, as previously seen, is also linked to OCD. We know that there is a definite interaction between glucose and L-Tryptophan. Glucose impairment has also been observed in the brains of patients with OCD. Therefore, if the OCD patient has a glucose impairment, it might be wise to prescribe a complex carbohydrate diet. The proper diet emphasizes the need to eat carbohydrates found in cereals, vegetables, salads, and fruits. This diet would also restrict the use of industrialized sugars, such as the ones found in cakes, pastries, ice cream, and candy.

For OCD patients with symptoms of hyperactive behavior, other dietary measures might be helpful. A hyperactive individual usually shows increased mental and physical activity and has difficulty concentrating, a short attention span, an inability to sit still, and an urge to be on the go. These patients usually have a very active mind, and their thoughts may race. They should suppress or decrease their consumption of sugars, caffeinated beverages, chocolate, and alcohol and look into a restricted monoamine diet (see table 7 – 3). Food containing large amounts of serotonin, such as bananas, might be helpful. Because some drugs may produce a vitamin depletion, vitamin supplements might be indicated.

Drug Interaction

Two drugs given at the same time might compete with each other, cancel out each other's actions, potentiate the action of each other, or cause side effects. If you have questions or hesitations about taking two drugs, ask your doctor.

SIDE EFFECTS

Medication side effects cause various degrees of discomfort that the patient may have to accept in order to control OCD symptoms. If side effects become intolerable or harmful, obviously medications should be discontinued. Because most OCD medications act upon the same brain chemistry or because they have the same family background, we expect to find similar side effects. Therefore, before switching drugs, it is best to see if another drug will indeed have different side effects.

Just as we all have different faces that distinguish us from one another, our biochemical profiles are also unique. Consequently, it is difficult to predict which side effects a patient will develop. Most side effects occur at the beginning of treatment, and gradually they disappear as the body gets used to the medication. Side effects might be avoided by starting treatment with very small doses of medication, or when indicated, by giving the medication at nighttime. By taking the medication at night, a higher drug blood level will be reached while the patient is sleeping. In this way, if any side effect occurs, it might go unnoticed. Drugs used for the treatment of OCD sometimes might be given in one single dose. The blood levels may remain considerably high during a twenty-four-hour cycle.

Drowsiness. Drowsiness is a common side effect that appears at the beginning of treatment. Once the body gets used to the drug, drowsiness usually disappears. Conversely, drowsiness may also appear after an increase in medication. In this case, if the symptom persists, the dose should be lowered.

Dry Mouth. Dry mouth is another common side effect. If the condition is disturbing, it can be relieved by taking small sips of water or by chewing gum. Severe dry mouth may also be controlled by giving urocholine.

Nausea. Nausea can be prevented by taking the medication on a full stomach.

Stomach Pains. Patients taking Prozac (fluoxetine) complain primarily of stomach pains, abdominal cramps, or generalized abdominal distress. These symptoms can be quite annoying, and if medications given to counteract them have no effect, dosage level may be altered. If these adjustments fail, treatment should be discontinued.

Constipation. For constipation, a diet based on salads, vegetables, and fruits might be helpful. Fruit juices, primarily prune juice, can be beneficial. Bran is also helpful. The goal is to increase bulk and water availability in the bowel. If the diet is unsuccessful, stool softeners might be used.

Blurred Vision. Blurred vision is caused by the loss of the eye's ability to focus its lens to different distances. Eye muscles may be weakened by the administration of medicines. If a patient needs to change his or her eyeglass prescription, the ophthalmologist should be told what medication the patient is on.

Delayed Urination. Some patients complain of difficulties with voiding. Others wake up more than once in the middle of the night to urinate. Delayed urination seen in prostate conditions may worsen with the administration of antidepressants.

Menstrual Changes. Generally, the menstrual cycle is not altered. Nonetheless, amenorrhea, or lack of menstruation, has been reported. Discontinuation of the drugs brings the menstrual cycle back to order.

Lactation. In very rare instances, spontaneous production of milk has been reported.

Weight Gain. With medicines for the mind, weight gain may be a problem. Patients on antidepressants may add an extra three to five pounds. In exceptional cases we have seen weight increases of up to forty pounds. A patient may say, "I am putting weight on, yet I eat as usual" or "I am always hungry" or "I have developed a craving for sweets." Weight gain is probably caused by changes in the functioning of the body or by a reduction in the symptoms of OCD. A slow burning of food intake may explain why patients put on weight without overeating. An increase or an overuse of sugar may be the culprit for craving sweets or feeling hungry. Hunger can also be explained by the action of the medication on the brain center that controls appetite.

Anxiety, tension, depression, and obsessions are symptoms that may influence the desire to eat. Therefore, an improvement of these symptoms will result in a change of appetite. For those with fear of contamination, including handling of food or eating in public places, a decrease in these fears will allow the patients to be in contact with food again, thus reflected in the increase in weight.

If weight gain produces health or aesthetic problems, some action should be taken. Patients may follow a low-calorie diet accompanied by an exercise program. The best exercises are aerobics; of those the most practical is brisk walking.

Weight Loss. Antidepressants that specifically increase serotonin availability may cause weight loss, with the exception of Anafranil®. For instance, fluoxetine has been reported to be an appetite suppressant in doses well above eighty milligrams, although even lower doses may have the same effect.

Psychiatric Side Effects. Ironically, medications geared to improve mental disorders may produce the opposite effect. The following is a description of some psychiatric and neurological side effects.

Nervousness. Nervousness, jitteriness, jumpiness, and restlessness are terms indicating an overstimulation of the nervous system. Antidepressants are expected to have a stimulant effect, or "pep" action. Antidepressants improve moods, accelerate thinking processes, and increase motor activity. While these properties are desirable, sometimes an overresponse occurs. When this takes place, the patient may go into a manic state characterized by a racing mind, fast speech, loss of appetite, excessive energy, and diminished need to sleep. Minor tranquilizers bring nervousness under control.

Anxiety. Anxiety has also been reported as a side effect. Because anxiety is one of the main secondary symptoms of OCD, an increase in anxiety caused by medication will undoubtedly affect therapy. Manipulation of medication dosage or the addition of an anti-anxiety agent may favorably resolve the problem, however.

Calmness. One drug used for OCD, Desyrel® (trazodone), has been reported to produce excessive tranquility or calmness, also accompanied by sleepiness. Sometimes, the use of L-Tryptophan may produce tiredness or excessive relaxation that may interfere with the patient's functioning.

Sleep Disturbances. Sleep changes may occur with OCD medications. Some patients report an increase in their sleeping time; others report an improvement of their sleeping pattern. Some patients develop insomnia. Insomnia means not only difficulty in falling asleep, but also frequent awakening during the night or early awakening, with an inability to fall asleep again. Insomnia is treated with sleeping pills. Sleeping medications are effective for about ten days, and after that their effect weakens.

In lieu of sleeping medication, L-Tryptophan may induce sleep in doses from one to two grams. Doses higher than two grams will be ineffective. As previously mentioned, Desyrel® (trazodone) may induce sleep. On the other hand, Prozac® (fluoxetine) may cause insomnia and should therefore be given in the morning.

Tremor. Tremor is a common side effect. Its intensity may become annoying if it becomes noticeable or interferes with work or the handling of objects. In general, tremor caused by medication is not severe: it may be continuous or appear intermittently. Patients with OCD who already have tremors caused by nervousness should not confuse this with the medicine's side effect. When tremors become severe, drug dosage should be reduced or discontinued altogether.

Loss of Balance. High doses of antidepressants may also cause loss of balance, mainly in older people.

Blood Pressure Changes. In general, blood pressure drops with the use of antidepressants. The change is mild and does not interfere with functioning. In some patients, the drop might be related to postural changes, such as when getting up from bed or from a chair or when bending down to pick up something from the floor. This is known as postural hypotension. But patients on MAOI may suffer from attacks of high blood pressure that are sometimes triggered by the patient's failure to follow the prescribed special diet.

Heart Rate. Antidepressants may increase the number of heartbeats per minute (tachycardia). Sometimes these drugs will induce missed beats. Periodic control of blood pressure and pulse, as well as evaluation of electrocardiogram tracings, might help to monitor such cardiovascular problems.

Sexual Dysfunction. A variety of sexual disturbances may occur during the administration of antidepressants, primarily loss of libido, a decrease or loss of orgasm, and male impotence. Yet some males complain of delayed ejaculation, a plus for those suffering from premature ejaculation. Some patients will complain of their inability to ejaculate. One serious, yet rare, side effect, continuous penis erection, can be caused by Desyrel® (trazodone). Such a continuous and painful erection may require surgery. Patients who are given this drug should be told in advance of this possible side effect.

Allergic Reactions. Allergic reactions, consisting of rashes and itching, can occur. Sometimes this rash looks like small pimples. Occasionally, allergies produce hives. Antiallergic medication can take care of the problem. If the allergic reaction is very strong, the medication should be discontinued.

MINOR TRANQUILIZERS

Minor tranquilizers are drugs used to treat anxiety, irritability, panic attacks, phobias, and alcohol withdrawal. These drugs are usually ineffective in the treatment of OCD but helpful in alleviating some of the OCD symptoms, such as anxiety, tension, nervousness, phobias, and panic attacks.

The most frequently used minor tranquilizers belonging to the benzodiazepine group are alprazolam, diazepam, clorazepate, dipotassium, lorazepam, oxazepam, halazepam, and prazepam.

The side effects of minor tranquilizers include drowsiness, fatigue, slow reflexes, loss of coordination, loss of balance, lack of concentration, memory impairment, and even anger.

You may not mix minor tranquilizers with alcohol, because serious side effects or even death may occur. Long-term use of these drugs, at high or even low dosages, may cause physical addiction. Sudden discontinuation of these drugs may cause withdrawal symptoms. These symptoms include jitteriness, sweating, nausea, vomiting, abdominal cramps, and convulsions. Therefore, drug withdrawal should be done gradually. At times, a different drug with fewer withdrawal side effects is used as part of a replacement therapy. Withdrawal should be medically supervised.

HYPNOTIC MEDICATION

Sleeping medication is usually given to patients with OCD who are chronic insomniacs. Some of these patients suffer from severe obsessions that keep them awake. The therapeutic efficacy of hypnotics lasts about ten days; thereafter, they become less effective. The most frequently used hypnotics are flurazepam, triazolam, quazepam, and temazepam. The old-timers are barbiturates, such as phenobarbital, secobarbital, and chloral hydrate.

Their side effects are next-morning hangover, forgetfulness, drowsiness, and tiredness. They may also cause difficulty breathing or skin allergies. In elderly people, agitation may be reported.

All hypnotics can cause physical dependency. Because of their side effects, one should be careful when driving, operating machinery, or performing duties where concentration is needed.

ANTICONVULSANT MEDICATION

Anticonvulsants are drugs used for the treatment of epileptic or seizure disorders. Patients with OCD and seizures may benefit from the administration of anti–obsessive-compulsive agents combined with anticonvulsants. Clonazepam, for example, has been used to treat anxiety, panic disorders, phobias, and mania.

Some side effects to watch for if pursuing this treatment are drowsiness, fatigue, and loss of coordination.

Factors to Take into Consideration before Taking a Drug

Weight. Medications are prescribed by body weight; the heavier the person, the higher the dose.

Age. Children and the elderly require similar dosages of medication. In children, paradoxical effects might occur. That is, a tranquilizer may cause excitation, while a stimulant may cause inhibition or depression. This can occur with Ritalin, a stimulant used to tranquilize hyperactive children.

In older people, these drugs may cause loss of balance, dizziness, or unsteady gait, resulting in falls that can cause fractures.

Alcohol. Alcoholic beverages are forbidden with the use of drugs for the brain. Alcohol may enhance the action of depressant drugs or tranquilizers. When alcohol is combined with antidepressants, violent behavior might be triggered. Combined side effects include drowsiness, dizziness, inability to concentrate, tremor, diarrhea, weak reflexes, fatigue, and even death.

Drug Abuse. Those who abuse drugs face problems similar to those who are alcoholics. Cocaine, a very strong mind stimulator, has many psychiatric side effects. Hallucinations, paranoia, moodiness, depression, suicidal and homicidal behavior, aggression, tension, anxiety, and loss of judgment are some of the symptoms experienced by cocaine addicts.

Similar side effects have been found with users of amphetamines, speed, or psychostimulants in general. Good-quality marijuana may cause hallucinations, paranoia, time dysperception, and depression.

For those using psychedelic drugs such as LSD, angel dust, mushrooms, and the like, psychiatric side effects are the norm.

There are anecdotal reports stating that LSD, cocaine, and marijuana have relieved OCD symptoms. Certainly, the damage caused by these substances outweighs their benefits. If you are using illegal drugs or alcohol, you should inform your doctor.

Drug abuse is not only unhealthy, but it will also certainly interfere with the treatment of OCD. We have found this to be true over and over again.

Use of Psychostimulants. Medications that boost the brain's energy, such as amphetamines and methylphenidate (Ritalin), have been employed in OCD treatment. Overall, they are ineffective and can aggravate OCD.

MAJOR TRANQUILIZERS

Major tranquilizers are drugs used to treat acute psychosis, schizophrenia, manic illness, and aggressive behavior. In small doses, these drugs have been used to treat most psychiatric disorders, including OCD. Major tranquilizers used to treat OCD have included perphenazine, properiazine, haloperidol, thioproperazine, thioridazine, chlorpromazine, thiothixene, and trifluoperazine.

Generally, major tranquilizers are no longer prescribed for the treatment of OCD. Results of their use have been equivocal. The new anti – obsessive-compulsive agents offer a better therapeutic outcome.

Polipharmacy. Polipharmacy is a term used by psychopharmacologists when more than one medication is used to treat a disease. Sometimes, when one single drug treatment fails, combining two or more drugs may be helpful. Also, if a medication to treat OCD causes anxiety, then a medication to treat the anxiety may also be necessary.

Physical Exercise. Anxiety and tension found in patients with OCD may cause lower back and neck pain, teeth grinding or clenching, and generalized or partial muscle contraction. Sometimes these conditions are chronic. Because of muscle contractions patients can change body posture, unaware that they are doing so. These postural changes will cause different muscles to contract or to relax in order to readjust to the new body position.

A vicious cycle then develops, a cycle that is difficult to interrupt. Consequently, more anxiety develops, and so forth.

A twenty-three-year-old woman came for a consultation because of severe OCD with fears of contamination. Her fears were so severe that eventually she became a prisoner in her room, which was furnished with only a bed and a chair. She refused to leave her house because she couldn't touch doorknobs. She considered most rooms of her house contaminated. Three items were not contaminated: her bedroom, her bed, and one chair. She used that chair to sit in most of the time when she was not in her bed. In order to decrease physical contact or to avoid touching contaminated objects (practically everything else in the whole house), she physically tried to shrink herself by walking with small steps, clenching her fists, crossing her arms, and lowering her head to touch her chest. As a result, she developed serious muscle contractions that required physical therapy to restore normal functioning.

Muscle tension, a symptom of anxiety, can be treated by physical exercises and/or relaxation exercises. Yoga, swimming, stretching exercises, and aerobics are excellent tools, provided that they are performed on a regular basis.

A few patients suffering from anxiety may worsen their anxiety by doing aerobic exercises, however. If this is true for you, then try stretch exercises, relaxation techniques, or yoga before and after aerobics. This approach might prevent an anxiety attack before or after exercising.

Electroshock Therapy. Electroconvulsive therapy is ineffective for the treatment of OCD. Sometimes it can produce transient improvement, but it is followed by a relapse and as such should probably be contraindicated.

Drug Therapy. Drug therapy aims to control the illness. Specifically, the goal is to suppress the symptoms; that is, to decrease the frequency, intensity, and duration of the symptoms and to control the anxiety, depression, and anger that accompany OCD.

We know we have accomplished our mission when the patient can function once again. We've succeeded when the patient can relate emotionally to others in a positive way, socialize, work, attend school, and engage in leisure activities.

What Your Doctor Wants to Know
Before Starting Drug Therapy

Do you
  suffer from allergies?
  have a serious heart problem or irregular heartbeats?
  suffer from low or high blood pressure?
  have a serious liver or kidney impairment?
  have a chronic lung condition?
  have a thyroid condition?
  have a peptic ulcer?
  have a history of convulsions or seizures?
  have tics or muscle twitches?
  suffer from irritable bowel syndrome?
  suffer from constipation?
  suffer from chronic diarrhea?
  suffer from indigestion?
  suffer from prostate enlargement or inflammation?
  have menstrual disturbances?
  have sexual disorders?
  suffer from alcoholism?
  suffer from drug addiction?
  have or have you had any major illnesses?
  suffer from acute narrow angle glaucoma?
Are you pregnant or trying to become pregnant?

How long does it take to know whether a drug will work? It takes from three to eight weeks to notice drug action on the symptoms. When medication is gradually increased to achieve therapeutic levels, it may take longer. In general, if a drug doesn't work within three months, chances of later improvement are slim.

How long does a patient stay on a drug? When the drug is effective, the patient should remain on that drug for at least three to six months after the improvement was first obtained. When optimal improvement has been reached, the drug dose may be lowered, until a minimal dose with the highest response level has been obtained. This is known as the *maintenance dose.* Some patients may have to stay on a maintenance dose for a longer period of time because symptoms may come back without medication.

TOXIC EFFECTS OF DRUGS

Prolonged administration of high or low doses of medication may impair bodily functions. Laboratory tests are available to keep an eye on bodily functions. Screen blood tests for liver, kidney, thyroid, blood count, and urinalysis should be requested periodically. Cardiovascular activity can be monitored by checking the blood pressure and pulse and by doing electrocardiogram tracings. Before starting drug therapy, a brain-wave test (EEG) may detect a seizure, convulsive disorder, or possible abnormal trends that may contraindicate the use of certain medications.

PSYCHOSURGERY

Patients should undergo psychosurgery only if all available treatments have failed and if the patient is severely incapacitated. Moreover, the decision should be made on an individual basis.

Psychosurgery seems more effective for compulsions. It is more difficult to eradicate obsessions with psychosurgery; however, psychosurgery may blunt their effect and dull the patient's mood so that he or she becomes indifferent to the OCD symptoms. Age at the time of surgery is irrelevant to a therapeutic outcome, but long illness evolution and duration make a favorable outcome less probable. Lastly, symptoms may recur after psychosurgery. Behavior therapy after psychosurgery is sometimes recommended.

I masturbate all day long. I listen to the radio. I drink alcohol. It helps for a while, then it starts all over again.

I have enough pain with my illness, and you want me to suffer more by having to take medication, talk nonsense about my problems, and only wash my hands a couple of minutes a day? Get out of here, will you? You make me sick. . . .

When he came to my office he checked behind my chair, I checked behind my chair. He checked underneath my desk, I checked underneath my desk. He checked inside all my books, I checked inside all my books. Then we looked at each other, and we both laughed. Believe it or not, his double-checking improved considerably shortly thereafter.

8

In-patient versus Out-patient Treatment

Hospital Treatment

We think most patients do not ask whether they should be hospitalized because they don't realize that hospitalization is a possibility. Treatment options should always be discussed with patients and a decision mutually reached as to the most favorable form of treatment for them at that particular time. Whether the treatment should be conducted on an out-patient or in-patient basis is an important question. The following factors should be considered when thinking about hospitalization:

Training of support staff

Patient's level of functioning

Patient's support system

Necessity to monitor treatment closely

Need for additional treatment

TRAINING OF SUPPORT STAFF

The support staff's knowledge about OCD, its treatment, and handling OCD patients is very important since they spend most of the time with the patient. Nurses, social workers, and occupational/art therapists should all be familiar with the treatment. This is especially important if the patient is undergoing intense behavioral treatment. Otherwise, the staff may hinder progress when trying to be helpful. For example, they may provide reassurance, although the therapist may be trying to get the patient to stop asking repetitive questions, to rely on his or her own decisions, or to take risks. The patient should inquire whether staff members are trained to deal with OCD and what their role will be during therapy. For instance, we always include the adjunct staff to help with exposure and response prevention (exposing patients to their fears and preventing them from engaging in compulsions). They become an extension of the therapist when the therapist is not available.

Patient's Level of Functioning

Many patients have reported that their symptoms become so overwhelming that they are practically immobilized within a particular section of the house. They designate a certain area of the house "safe" from asbestos, radiation, chemicals, or myriad other things. Any departure from the "safe area" within the house would immediately put them in contact with extremely feared objects or situations. In the hospital, though, patients often report a feeling of starting afresh.

For many patients, the house may be the main area where their symptoms occur. For others, the house is their haven. Their level of functioning is severely limited outside, but not inside, the house. For example, a patient suffering from fears of contamination may be able to do everything within the house, as long as the groceries are washed, immediate family members change their clothes, and everyone follows the set of rules dictated by the patient. Outside the house, the patient may not be able to function at all. In fact, the patient may be functioning in the house because the family structure and environment have been greatly modified, allowing the patient to avoid most feared items and situations.

In the hospital, the patient is prevented from avoiding feared items and situations. Consequently, these patients may realize the severity of their disorder only when hospitalized.

PATIENT'S SUPPORT SYSTEM

We all need support whenever we start something new and frightening. Patients also need tender loving care during treatment. Some patients lack this support at home. In addition, if the patient is receiving behavioral treatment, there may be no one to serve as a *co-therapist*. A co-therapist is one who assists the therapist by helping the patient practice his or her behavioral assignments between sessions.

In a hospital setting, the adjunct staff, providing they comprehend the various facets of the disorder, can serve as co-therapists and provide an open ear. In addition to the staff, other patients may also reach out to OCD patients and help them overcome their fears.

In most hospitals there are morning meetings during which the new patient is introduced to the community. At the meeting, the patient's symptoms are explained to the rest of the patients. This provides the hospital community with an understanding of the new patient's treatment and needs while in the hospital. We have found that the support of other patients has often enabled OCD patients to face their fears and do their behavioral assignments. Later on, we will further discuss how support systems aid in the treatment of patients.

NECESSITY TO MONITOR TREATMENT CLOSELY

At times, behavioral and drug therapies require close monitoring. For those patients who respond poorly to medication, changes can be made in their medications while the staff watches for side effects. Patients with physical disorders, such as a heart condition, may need to be closely monitored, especially if the medication affects cardiac activity. Patients going through a behavioral program may need supervision in resisting their obsessions or compulsions. In addition, some patients may be so eager to improve that they will attempt to push themselves beyond their limits. The nursing staff could monitor their actions and, if need be, slow them down. Sometimes it's important for the therapist to observe the patient's obsessive-compulsive behavior, reactions to others, interactions, sleeping and eating habits, and many other such habits that may not be feasible on an out-patient basis.

NEED FOR ADDITIONAL TREATMENT

In the hospital setting, patients can deal with their family problems, marital issues, self-esteem, negative feelings, traumas, and so forth. These problems are brought up and discussed in a safe setting. Since the OCD is usually very absorbing, out-patient therapy rarely affords sufficient time to discuss these issues until treatment of OCD is terminated. In an in-patient unit, the therapist and the psychiatrist can conduct therapy and treatment geared specifically toward the obsessive-compulsive symptoms, while the rest of the staff can begin to help the patient cope with other problems.

While we have mainly discussed compulsive individuals, obsessional people should not be neglected. Patients who primarily have obsessions may also need hospitalization. Obsessions may limit patients' functioning, and the severity may be such that they cannot cope or engage in any other activity. They may be continuously preoccupied with their own thoughts. They need to learn to be more outer directed, in other words, outside of themselves. The hospital setting is perfect for this, since patients are encouraged to participate in various activities and to discuss issues in a group with the staff.

HOW THE HOSPITAL STAFF CAN HELP

Assuming that the doctor and patient decide on hospitalization, the next question is, How can the patient take the best advantage of a hospital stay? The nursing staff, if they have been trained to work with OCD patients, can be of tremendous help. Even in cases when the patient is receiving only drug treatment, the nursing staff can notice changes in the patient's symptomatology, and this can enhance the efficacy of drug administration. Side effects reported by the patient may be common during the initial phases of treatment, and the nursing staff can help the patient to tolerate these side effects while adjusting to the medication. The nursing staff may also alert the psychiatrist to make certain dosage modifications so that the patient can tolerate the medication until it can later be increased.

Patients in therapy on an out-patient basis may too readily give up a medication, wrongly assuming they will always experience side effects. Most medications have what is called a *thera-*

peutic window, the dosage level where the medication is most effective, and the psychiatrist aims to bring the patient to that level to realize optimum benefit of the prescribed drug.

In the case of behavior therapy, the nursing staff can again be of enormous help to the therapist. Generally, patients are given homework assignments after their daily sessions. These homework assignments are geared toward having the patient practice what he or she learned during the therapy session. The nursing staff can help the patient do the homework assignments.

The staff may show patients who are washers how to wash in a normal fashion and how to time showers. Initially, many patients have difficulty taking a ten-minute shower, not being accustomed to it. The staff may go in every few minutes to inform the patient how many more minutes are left and tell him or her what to do in order to complete the shower within the prescribed time period.

Modeling—having the therapist illustrate what he or she wants the patient to do—is very helpful to many patients. For example, if the patient is a collector, it is useful to watch the therapist or others actually throw things out. If the patient is a checker, the therapist and staff can demonstrate how they would hang up a phone or walk out of a room without checking the door or electric switches several times. During modeling and observing other people, patients can see how others think and how their beliefs help them function differently from themselves.

In the case of obsessional patients who have an urge to be reassured repeatedly, the nursing staff teaches them how to overcome the problem by denying reassurance. We have found that the nursing staff can do this rather easily, while family members cannot. Family members very often give in to the patient's demands for several reasons:

They tire easily because they have been exposed to the problem for a long time.

Their familiarity with the patient leads to discomfort when resisting the patient's repetitive questioning.

Their resistance more readily lends itself to arguments.

Family members feel they cannot be "cruel" to the patient.

We tell patients that they will be denied reassurance by the staff and that this is necessary for recovery. Obsessional patients who resort to telephone calling to alleviate their obsessions are prevented from making phone calls. They are allowed neither to have phones in their rooms nor initially to make outgoing calls without supervision.

Other patients with morbid obsessions, such as hurting others, may be encouraged to act out their fears in order to learn that they will not carry out their obsessions. This type of therapy of exposing patients to their fears is known as *flooding*.

Kenny was a twenty-five-year-old patient who had a fear of stabbing others with sharp objects. He used to hide all the knives, scissors, and screwdrivers in his house. If he ever got the courage to use a knife, he would immediately wash it and put it away. In the hospital, we had Kenny walk around with knives, use them in the presence of other patients, and toward the end of his treatment put the knife right against our backs, urging him to stab us. Of course, we knew he would never do it, but we had to prove it to him. After quite a bit of practice with knives, scissors, and the various utensils used in occupational therapy, his obsessions decreased and he was no longer frightened of acting out his urges.

Patients who haven't cooked in a long time because they're afraid of contaminating others are encouraged to cook for the whole staff without washing. We often take patients to supermarkets and have them touch cleaning items and then purchase vegetables and fruits. We then have them serve fruit salads or other foods to the staff. All this is done in an attempt to teach patients that what they fear will not occur.

Many patients have difficulty touching other people, and, in fact, they may be limited to touching one or two people within their own family. We get these patients gradually to touch the staff and other patients within the hospital. Thereafter, we encourage them to wait and see whether the people get sick or die during their hospitalization.

Many compulsions can be controlled during hospitalization. For instance, patients who use toilet paper, tissues, or wipes excessively can be restricted in their usage merely by making these items inaccessible. Toilet paper can be administered as necessary and in limited quantities to prevent patients from using it to clean themselves excessively.

Pamela and Franklyn were in the hospital at the same time and with the same problem. They each spent an average of one and a half hours urinating, defecating, and wiping themselves each morning. They would then try to hold their urge to go to the bathroom again until the next morning. Otherwise, it would mean spending another one and a half hours and then changing clothes. It was easier in the morning, because after wiping themselves, they would shower and spend approximately fifteen minutes washing their genitals. Then they would put on clean clothes. If they had to go to the bathroom during the day, it would mean touching their genitals and buttocks, and then, in their minds, spreading urine and feces all around. It was impossible for them to entertain the idea of going to the bathroom and not showering or putting on clean clothes. Both Pam and Frank went through a bar of soap and a roll of toilet paper every two days. They confided that on several occasions they had urinated in their pants because they could not hold it anymore.

In the hospital, we gave them small bars of soap (the kind one gets at a hotel), and asked them to use as little as possible. Each day they would return the unused portion to the staff, in order for us to monitor the amount used. The hospital staff gave them the normal amount of toilet paper, and all other papers and tissues were removed from their rooms. We did not allow them to shower daily. We had them touch their buttocks, walk barefoot on the grass, where there might be urine or feces from animals, touch toilet flushes, and have their legs touch the toilet bowl edge without washing their hands or bodies. We exposed them to their fears and prevented them from washing. This therapy, as we mentioned earlier, is known as exposure and response prevention. In two months they were able to do all these things without any problems. They were discharged.

Of course, it is necessary for the nursing staff to understand the problem, since merely removing toilet paper and other items is not sufficient. At first, for example, the toilet paper must be removed without contaminating other objects. The patient may be allowed to put the items in a "clean" bag and remove them, when needed, under the supervision of the nursing staff. As treatment progresses, patients are encouraged to function independently of the staff's supervision. The toilet paper, regular bar of soap, and tissues are kept in the patient's room, and they are asked to control the use of these items on their own.

The hospital should be a place where patients feel comforttable discussing their anxieties and learn how to reduce them. They should be able to learn how to change their beliefs about their feared items, objects, situations, and/or people. Usually the staff is immediately available as the problem arises, whereas at home, family or friends may not be. Generally, by the time patients seek treatment, seven to ten years have elapsed since the onset of the disorder, and many patients have lost their friends. The seriousness of their problems and their inability to relate to others usually causes friendships to break up. Family members with a low tolerance threshold may get angry more quickly when a problem arises and thereby can't provide a supportive environment. In the hospital, other patients can be supportive since they, too, need support during their hospitalization, and they understand the suffering and ostracism.

Within the family setting, the following scenario usually occurs. The patient has a problem with a particular situation, person, or thought. He or she then seeks aid from a family member, who may initially try to reason with the patient, but then becomes frustrated and angry. The anger elicits more anxiety in the patient, the problem grows, the family member becomes more frustrated and angry, the patient becomes more anxious, and a vicious cycle develops. At times the cycle is difficult to break.

PROBLEMS ENCOUNTERED PRIOR TO HOSPITALIZATION

Assuming that hospitalization is desirable, there are certain problems that may arise before going to the hospital. These problems are specific to patients with fears of contamination. The hospital is one of the biggest sources of contamination for them; thus they greatly desire to avoid the hospital. For patients with OCD, the hospital is perceived not as a place of sterility, cleanliness, and safety, but rather as a place that is very dangerous, where they can contract various illnesses and/or harm others who are vulnerable.

The most frequently asked question is whether a patient will have a private room. It is not so much a desire for privacy that prompts the request, rather a wish to have the least amount of contamination in the room. Sharing a room with another patient means being exposed to many feared objects. Patients with OCD would like to sterilize their private rooms and keep them sterilized rather than expose themselves and, in their minds, contract myriad diseases, such as AIDS, herpes, venereal diseases, hepatitis, cancer, leukemia, and the like. Using hospital sheets, drawers, and bathroom facilities is another problem. But the anticipatory anxiety is generally greater than the actual anxiety experienced in the real situation.

Most patients can touch and put their clothes in the drawers and closet if the therapist works with them. Most patients with OCD ask if they can bring their own sheets and blankets. This is not advisable because the object of therapy is to get the patient accustomed to behaving like others. If these issues deter patients from checking into the hospital, however, we usually allow patients some avoidance behaviors, such as using their own sheets until they can mentally handle it.

Out-patient Treatment

Most of this chapter has dealt with the benefits of hospitalization because patients know very little about what to expect in a hospital. Certainly most of us know a lot more about going to an office for treatment.

There are benefits to being treated on an out-patient basis. First of all, patients are in the environment that elicits most of their problems. If a patient doesn't need or refuses hospitalization for whatever reason, treatment can be initiated in the office. On an out-patient basis, patients can be exposed to the daily activities with which they may have difficulty coping. For example, if they have contamination fears, we go to the specific restaurants, grocery stores, shops, streets, and neighborhoods where patients encounter their problems. Most patients have difficulty doing tasks in their own homes, such as laundry, cleaning, cooking, walking out of the house without double-checking, putting their "contaminated" and "noncontaminated" clothes together, and so on. For patients who have hoarded various items in their homes, it is necessary to work with them to throw out these things gradually. In addition, since patients will be exposed to their fears daily in their homes, their anxieties may be alleviated quicker. While out-patient treatment may be a plus in some instances, it is not the only way to obtain benefits from therapy. Sometimes hospitalization may be required. When choosing between home, out-patient, or hospital treatment, weigh the benefits and detriments of being treated in each place.

What have you been doing all this time, just making money on people's suffering? I am sorry, doc. Now let me cry.

Why me, doctor? I don't care that millions of people have OCD.

Hey, wait a minute, I'm not planning to come back. Just give me the prescription and call my drugstore once a month, for renewals. . . .

My rituals upon awakening take about three hours of my time. You have to add another three hours before going to bed.

9

The Social Scene

M ARY, thirty-five years of age, underwent behavioral and drug therapy and improved quite a bit. She had never dated because of her illness, however, and was frightened of this prospect. She didn't know how to kiss, how to hold a man's hand in the movies, or how to act at the end of a date. We tried our best to instruct her as we challenged her faulty beliefs that she had to be perfect, that she couldn't handle rejection, that everyone would reject her, and that she didn't dare make mistakes. But she was still fearful.

Mary never took an interest in sex during early adolescence, and by the end of high school, her symptoms had begun. Although she went on to college and developed superficial relationships, she spent most of her working hours catering to her symptoms, and in between she studied. She desperately wanted to get married and have children, but even when she had an occasional date, her anxiety would prevail, and she inevitably would say or do the wrong thing. For example, she would pay attention to others rather than her date, jump out of the car almost before her date would stop, and forget to tell him she had had a nice evening and would like to see him again.

Bradley was fifty-five and had been a loner most of his life. He spoke to his coworkers at the print shop but didn't know how to ask them to go for a beer after work. For many years he had suffered with OCD and had done his best to stay away from others for fear of being discovered. OCD is a hidden illness, and people usually are embarrassed by the symptoms. As the years went on, Bradley was getting tired of being alone, but he didn't know how to socialize.

Anna was a thirty-five-year-old mother of three who had divorced when her husband could no longer live with her symptoms. She overcame the disorder but still lost her husband and friends after the divorce. She started working, but it was hard to make new friends. She didn't know whether she should inform her new friends about her disorder, which occasionally would recur. Would her new friends reject her if they knew about her past? If she were to remarry, should she tell her future husband? Sometimes it seemed easier to sit home and watch television.

Tony, eighteen years old, kept going to the bathroom to wash his hands. Prior to the development of his OCD two years earlier he had had many friends. He was a popular athlete, and girls found him attractive. But now he couldn't even get a date for the prom. Everyone teased him. He tried desperately to hide his symptoms, but they were obvious to everyone. Tony couldn't get into other kids' cars. His friends didn't know that he thought their cars were contaminated by dirt. He walked around feeling dirty. His friends would throw things at him to see if he would pick them up. He couldn't, so he would try to ignore them or pretend he didn't see what they were doing. They would ask him why he didn't touch the floor, or why he didn't play baseball any longer, but he wouldn't answer. Tony would spend hours crying in his room at night, humiliated and alone.

Steve, twenty-two years of age, spent hours in the bathroom wiping himself, touching faucets in a particular way, and examining his hair to make sure it was properly placed. He even quit college to devote his time to these activities. He hated himself for it. He lost his self-respect. He was angry. He dropped his high-school girlfriend and his friends with no explanation. What could he say to them? Could he tell them that he had to wipe himself perfectly clean or had to keep cutting his hair until there wasn't a hair out of place? Finally, he shaved off his hair, but that didn't help either, because within a week it started to grow back. He didn't seek treatment for some time because of his shame.

Many OCD patients have severely impaired social relations or never learn necessary social skills because they spend many years catering to their particular symptoms. Some patients lose the few friends they do have because they are unable to continue the relationships; the fears or obsessions become too pervasive and interfere with every aspect of their lives.

In order to interact socially, gain friends, establish business relations, or date, sensitivity and social skills are necessary. Sensitivity and thoughtfulness allow us to become aware of the needs and feelings of others. We need to evaluate the priorities and limitations of others and learn to compromise our needs. A mutually trustworthy relationship must be developed. This requires an ability to know when to say what, how to say it, when to offer assistance, when to move away and give space to the other person, and how not to be self-absorbed.

A person with OCD requires the same qualities as anyone else in order to socialize. They include the following:

Social ease

Respect for others

Being attuned to others

Thoughtfulness

Patience

Understanding

Ability to compromise

Awareness

Responsibility

Loyalty

Many of our patients have serious difficulties establishing and maintaining relationships. It becomes very difficult for single patients to marry and for married patients to remain so. About half of the patients remain single, and half divorce.

It is quite difficult for patients with OCD to develop serious relationships or to grow with someone else. Their symptoms usually interfere with social adjustment. Friendships, as well as working relations, are strained.

In over seventeen years of working with OCD patients, we have found that they are socially isolated. They feel misunderstood, and their symptoms prevent them from reaching out to others. Compared to any other patient group, they probably suffer most from their isolation. They want to be with others, to do the same things, but they can't. The only other group of patients who can identify with their isolation are the agoraphobics who experience anxiety when out alone. Both groups want to be out, to do things and go places, but their symptoms won't allow it.

When their symptoms are treated, however, they have different problems to face. Mary, who had never dated, had to be taught how to spend an evening with a man. We gave her reading material to educate herself about her own sexuality. We encouraged her to put personal ads in the paper and to sign up with a dating agency. This was not an easy process. It took us several years to get her to feel at ease socially and to follow through on our suggestions. We were becoming as frustrated as she. One day she announced she was no longer going to try because her first three dates rejected her. We empathized with her. After all, it took a lot of courage and hard work to take the risk of dating, and to have three men not call her back must have been devastating. It's easy for us to say, What's three rejections? Life is full of rejection. Everyone gets rejected; it doesn't mean something's wrong with you. But if you were Mary, thirty-five and frightened of looking foolish, rejection is not the same experience. It took another couple of months to get Mary back on her feet and willing to try again. We were frightened for her. Eventually, she met a nice man whom she dated for a year, though they never married. She's still looking for her dream beau.

Should I tell others about my OCD? Patients always wonder whether they should tell new friends about their disorders. We advise patients to tell others about their illnesses, once the friendship is secured. We realize that in telling a prospective spouse or a friend, the patient risks losing that relationship. We recognize how hard it is to put oneself in that position, especially as in the case of Anna, whose husband divorced her because her symptoms became intolerable. Although after treatment she was not 100 percent cured, her obsessions and compulsions no longer interfered with her daily activities. Still, another man might be afraid they would come back. Anna couldn't tolerate the idea of another rejection.

We try to convince our patients that with time, it's best to let people know. If the love is strong enough, it will stand up to the past. Friends will try to understand. Our experience shows that most girlfriends, boyfriends, and friends accept OCD patients the way they are. Patients are not the illness; they *have* an illness. They have many things to offer. The illness is only an unfortunate eclipse in the life of the patient.

There you are. This is the blueprint of the location of my food in the refrigerator. Everything is in the right spot. If my children move the ketchup from its place, I surely punish them.

I like to be in control. If I lose my reason, I will not be in control.

The brain is not separated from the body. What occurs in the brain affects the body. What occurs in the body affects the brain. That is the reason we have a neck.

No, it hasn't affected my medical practice yet. However, being a surgeon I must be at work by 7:00 A.M. If I sleep, I don't socialize; if I socialize, I don't sleep. I only operate and ritualize.

10

The Family

T HE word *family* is derived from the Latin root *familia*, meaning servant. Certainly, this is not a flattering derivation for
an institution that we hold sacred. Are family members actually
servants of one another, and should the relationships be perceived as undesirable? We believe that members of a family do,
indeed, serve one another but, we hope, in a positive manner.

We are all dependent upon each other. The dependency increases when one suffers physical or mental disorders, and while
it is the family's obligation to serve the needs of the patient, they
do not have to be servants. In any healthy family environment,
there is interdependency among the members. The amount of
dependency varies, according to age, position within the family
structure, and well-being of the individual. OCD produces more
dependency and consumes more of the family's time and energy
than most disorders. Patients with OCD usually end up dominat-
ing the family, leading to endless struggles between the patient
and family, with the latter eventually resigning and giving in to
the demands of the patient. While this scenario sounds vicious, it
is the result of the illness, rather than the patient's desire to impose his or her will.

Unlike other disorders, such as depression, where the symptoms are limited to the patient, with OCD the symptoms are all-
encompassing. Very often, the compulsions involve family
members and the home itself. Obsessions, doubting, and indecisiveness also lead to family involvement.

Forty-two-year-old Frank never married and lived at home with
his mother, father, and brother Jim (thirty-five years old). Frank
could touch only his bed, one orange armchair, and a few paper

cups and plates in the kitchen. He considered the whole house contaminated, and certain rooms were kept locked in order to prevent the contamination from spreading. Because he feared germs, Frank stood up most of the day. Consequently, he developed swollen ankles owing to poor blood circulation. Frank also doubted everything and needed constant reassurance that he wasn't going to hurt the eight-year-old child across the street. Frank's parents eventually had to get rid of some furniture and be extremely careful not to touch Frank's belongings. If he suspected that any one of them had rubbed against his bed or chair, the furniture had to be washed thoroughly, and the family member had to take a decontaminating shower. Frank had worked as a schoolteacher until ten years earlier when he finally took a disability leave.

Until five years earlier, his sister Lucy also lived in the house. Lucy moved out because she could not tolerate the house and decided to remove herself from the "sickness of my family." She thought that would be her only salvation, although she could not very well afford living alone on a salesperson's salary. She decided to struggle rather than be completely controlled by Frank and see her parents "weak, submissive, and no longer in control of their own home." Lucy stated she lost respect for her parents and resented Frank. She could not see how Jim tolerated living in the house.

Jim had returned home after an unsuccessful marriage and was attending chiropractic school. Jim's personality was very different from Lucy's. He withdrew to his room and studied. He felt sorry for Frank and wanted to help him get over his problems. He understood his parents' predicament. At times Jim was also frustrated, angry, and jealous of the attention Frank got from his parents.

Frank didn't allow anyone in the house. His parents could not entertain and were allowed to socialize only with a few people. His parents quickly learned not to tell Frank about their evenings out, because inevitably he thought there was something wrong with the other couple (they were contaminated somehow), and they would have to end the friendship. If Frank heard his mother talking on the phone with someone he perceived as contaminated (which was almost everyone), he would have a crying or screaming fit.

Jim learned early on not to talk about school, or for that matter, any subject besides the weather and Frank's suffering. Periodically, when Frank had to get reassurance from Jim, he would barge into Jim's room in a state of panic, interrupt Jim, and begin questioning him. Jim would be patient at first. Then Frank would begin incessantly apologizing for interrupting and disturbing his studies. This could go on for two hours, during which time Jim was unable to study. Compulsive apologizing had become the symptom that most aggravated Jim.

Frank spent his days eating and watching television (standing up), which someone in the family had to turn on and off for him. He could not sit at the supper table; therefore his mother would prepare his meals by washing her hands thoroughly and then serving the food on paper goods. He would take his meal and eat it either standing up or occasionally putting it on the bed. Frank became very depressed. He enjoyed nothing. Simple routine behaviors became a chore. He avoided going to the bathroom and occasionally would even urinate or defecate in his pants. Going to the bathroom meant he would have to pull down his pants (which could take thirty minutes in itself), wipe himself (which could take up to one hour since he was never satisfied with his level of cleanliness), and then pull up his pants for thirty minutes. Two hours of sheer frustration was not something he could often tolerate.

On Frank's forty-second birthday his parents decided they could not let this continue any longer. They spoke to Frank and told him he had to go for treatment or move out. Frank opted for treatment with much reluctance and finally came to see us.

Not everyone's symptoms are as severe as Frank's. Regardless, the symptoms upset the whole family structure. Enabling a patient by performing rituals for him or her is not helpful in the long run. It's better to let the patient perform a ritual than to stop it. This rule is broken only when the therapist enlists a family member as a co-therapist and the patient agrees to allow a family member to attempt to stop him or her. Otherwise, attempts to stop the rituals will result in the patient's becoming more upset, thereby increasing the urge to perform the ritual. Obsessions also increase under anxiety or stress.

Main Problem Areas

There are three main areas that produce friction among patients and family members. Perhaps you will be able to recognize some of the problems that we are going to touch upon: repetitive questioning, self-absorption, and strange or bizarre rituals.

Because patients are uncertain, they are never sure that they understand instructions well or, for that matter, anything involving their memory. Chances are that their memory is fine and their problem is the need for reassurance. Therefore, they will repeat the same question over and over again to be certain that others understand them correctly.

OCD will eventually take over patients' entire lives and the lives of their families because the obsessions and compulsions are unrelenting. They become extremely preoccupied with their daily routine of having to cater to their illness. The patients become self-centered and self-absorbed and are unable to pay attention to the needs of others because they are too preoccupied with their obsessions and compulsions. In a "normal family" everyone gives and everyone receives, and the exchange continues. In the long run, the forced selfishness imposed on them by their illness may destroy the familial relationships they are seeking to maintain or establish. Loneliness sets in as they become ostracized.

Sometimes the behaviors are very bizarre. Here is an illustration.

In 1972, Nancy came from out of state to see us. She and her mother had driven a long way. Nancy walked into our office with a hat, shawl, gloves, and an overcoat. It didn't surprise us, because it was a rather cold winter morning. It was indeed a surprise when her mother had to take off her hat, shawl, gloves, and coat.

Nancy was a thirty-three-year-old housewife, married for about two years, with no children. Her husband was an insurance agent and was away most of the time. He would leave early in the morning and return home late in the evening, sometimes making frequent trips to neighboring towns.

Nancy indicated that her illness started at about age six, when she began school. She was frightened by having to go to school and by being separated from her mother. In order to control her fears, she developed a system of rituals. She had to touch a particular doll that she kept on a shelf in her bedroom, had to wear brown shoes every even day, and finally had to circle the dining-room table every night before going to sleep. When we asked her why she performed those rituals or activities, she didn't know. She did tell us that she had thought quite a few times about it, but couldn't come up with an answer. Eventually these symptoms went away.

About three months before she first menstruated, she began to obsess about cleanliness. She said perhaps this was a consequence of having been raised by a mother who was an extremely clean person. Her mother was very meticulous, orderly, rigid, and critical.

Later on, during her adolescent years, she became more concerned with thoughts that began to intrude into her consciousness without warning. Like other girls, she became interested in sex during adolescence. But she was also interested in aberrant sexual acts that horrified her. She never did anything "wrong" but was petrified that perhaps she could. She had ideas of performing sexual acts with men, women, and even children. She used to babysit, but she stopped because she was afraid she might sexually abuse little children.

Being brought up Catholic, she went to confession, and her priest reassured her that there was no sin in those types of thoughts, because they were temptations of the devil. He told her to pray to counteract the intrusion of the demon. She engaged in ritualistic praying and became quite religious, attending Mass every day.

At home, her mother still criticized her. She was never satisfied with her daughter's achievements in school, with the way she cleaned her bedroom, or with the way she groomed herself. Slowly, Nancy developed a tremendous sense of inadequacy. Her self-esteem dissipated. She was ashamed of herself. She felt insecure and, eventually, unable to make decisions.

She completed high school and took a secretarial position

after two years of training. At age twenty-two, when she found she was overweight, she decided not to eat. She became obsessed with food and with her body shape and considered herself extremely ugly. Consequently, she quit working. She lost about thirty pounds and decided she would eat only if her mother spoon-fed her. And so her mother did.

Nancy became almost paralyzed from any kind of activity. She refused to leave the house and had to be spoon-fed, bathed, and dressed every morning. During her menstrual period, her mother had to change her tampons. When things reached this point, a friend of the family suggested seeing a psychiatrist.

What is interesting in this family is that no one ever raised that question before. Were they embarrassed? Was a mental disorder a stigma to be kept hidden? A secret that cannot ever be revealed? With the help of psychotherapy and medication (probably for anxiety), Nancy improved enough to be able to go back to work, to date, and eventually to marry.

After two years of marriage, she developed new symptoms, such as double-checking and a complete inability to undertake household chores. So, every day when her husband went to work, her mother would walk in and take over the house, including the cleaning, shopping, laundry, and so forth. Just before coming to consult with us, the patient developed severe constipation and refused to clean herself following defecation, so her mother had to wipe her as well.

We can see in this case the incredible dependency on a family member. We also see the mother's tacit encouragement of this abnormal dependency. In cases like this one questions treatment outcome. Will her mother sabotage treatment? Although the patient may benefit by improving and gaining a sense of freedom, the mother may sustain the loss of being unable to continue dedicating her entire life to her daughter. After all, isn't this what she had done since Nancy was six years old?

Marital Difficulties

It is difficult to determine whether a marriage can survive the strains of OCD or other physical or mental illness. From 40 to 68 percent of OCD patients remain single. In most cases they were never married, so the relatively high incidence of singles doesn't seem to be a function of divorce. It appears that the symptoms prevent the individual from functioning, and therefore he or she cannot marry. More men than women are single. Traditionally, since more economic responsibility has been placed on men, they find it more difficult to assume the provider role and follow through with marriage.

Our experience shows most marriages are disturbed but do survive. Some spouses are more understanding than others, but few actually get divorced. Those who remain married usually build up anger over time. Initially, they are helpful and understanding. As the disorder persists, however, the spouse's response changes from indifference to extreme frustration and explosive behavior. Gradually, the relationship deteriorates. After the symptoms have been treated, marital therapy may help to restore the relationship.

AGGRESSION IN THE FAMILY

Of all the mental disorders, OCD is one of the most devastating and most frustrating illnesses for both the patient and the family. There isn't a single area of the patient's life that is not affected.

We found that approximately 65 percent of the patients report having one or more aggressive thoughts per week. Most patients, however, do not act aggressively unless there is outside interference with their compulsions. In addition, there seems to be a direct relationship between their anger and the severity of their symptoms. As the symptoms dissipate, so does the anger. While on the surface it makes sense that any patient with a disorder would feel angry with an illness and happy as he or she improved, we find this relationship to be more often true with OCD patients than with others. Although anger is not unique to OCD, it is certainly a predominant feeling with OCD patients. Serotonin, a neurotransmitter implicated in the etiology of OCD, is also known to regulate aggressive behavior. Perhaps this is why we see a stronger link between aggression and OCD symptoms.

We have observed the most gentle, soft-spoken patients exhibit cutting, spiteful behavior, and throw temper tantrums almost instantaneously, as if they were undergoing some form of transformation. They feel guilty afterward, although a strong sense of pride may prevent them from apologizing. Sometimes the patients do not recognize their aggression, although it is evident to the family and to us. It is manifested in backhanded compliments, "constructive criticism"; persistence in satisfying their needs while making others believe they are flexible; inability to empathize with the family's stress; inability to perceive situations from another person's point of view; and so on. Although these characteristics are not observed solely in patients with OCD, they are quite common. Whether these traits are linked to serotonin remains to be seen. But as the patient improves, so do these behaviors.

As mentioned elsewhere in this book, the families can also become prisoners of the disorder. It's not that the patient wants to enslave family members, but the disorder takes control and dictates how the patient and the family must live. If a family member rebels or refuses to give reassurance or to engage in a compulsion, aggressive behavior may erupt. The patient may become extremely frustrated and yell, scream, kick a piece of furniture, stomp his or her feet, or throw something. But it is usually the family members who physically attack the patient out of frustration to stop the patient's ritual or constant questioning and/or to procure their own freedom from obsessions and compulsions.

We do not condone aggression, yet we do understand why it occurs in families of patients with OCD. Through understanding we can make recommendations to our patients and their families on how to stop it.

Here are some suggestions to help the family through the crisis:

1. Let patients perform their compulsion, and do not try to stop it unless you are a co-therapist and the patient has previously agreed to your role.
2. Do not perform rituals for the patient or give reassurance.
3. Quietly state that you will not answer obsessional questions.
4. Leave the room or, if need be, the house when you are frustrated and think you are losing your patience.

5. Leave the patient in peace and quiet, since anxiety owing to families' interference will exacerbate the symptoms.
6. Do not ask questions once you return.

While these suggestions may prevent aggression, they do not necessarily help patients improve.

How to Help the Patient Who Refuses Help

A common problem encountered by some families is the fear of violence when a patient refuses treatment. Families ask us for guidance when a patient is reclusive in their home or in an apartment set up by the family. What should they do when their "patient" refuses to seek treatment? We usually recommend having one of our psychologists speak to the patient on the phone or meet him or her immediately outside the house. We've even had psychologists stand outside the home while the patient speaks through the door or window. Sometimes this works, but not all patients are amenable to these suggestions. Then we must work with the family.

It is important that the family not enable the patient by providing food or other necessities. Of course, families become concerned that the patient will become emaciated. If this occurs, then the local crisis unit, composed of a team of mental health professionals, should be called to the house to assess whether the patient needs help. Patients who are dangerous to themselves (unable to care for themselves) and/or to others are removed from the home and brought to the local hospital. From there they may be transferred immediately to a facility that can properly treat OCD.

Generally, we make arrangements with the family beforehand to have a bed available in our hospital in order to make a smooth and immediate transfer possible. Our experience shows that the patients truly want help and are grateful for the "push" that they couldn't muster themselves. Reclusive patients are generally extremely anxious and frightened, and it is for this reason they refuse voluntary treatment. Once help is there, they welcome it.

Most families are afraid that the patient will become violent if they impose treatment. Imposition of treatment must be presented with love and concern. The family's concern for the patient's welfare prompts this drastic step. They fear what will happen to the patient when they can no longer provide for him or her. The patient must be told of the family's love and unwillingness to watch him or her deteriorate or live a life of nonexistence. It must be emphasized that loved ones cannot stand around and watch someone die in front of their eyes and do nothing about it.

If the patient becomes violent, the most he or she will do is wreck the house. Leave the house and come back later. If possible, don't repair the damage. If this continues or escalates, let it. It stops after a few times. When families don't react, generally the aggression dies. Give it time. Stay calm and cool. Try to keep the interest of the patient in mind, and take action that will be of benefit in the long run.

We realize that our recommendations are hard and drastic, but sometimes there are no other options. We must work for the ultimate benefit of the patient.

Uncertainty is upsetting to me. It brings me anxiety. I need certainty. Doubting is killing me.

Explanations are not enough.

Happiness speeds up time. Depression slows it down. Happy people have a future. Depressed people have only their past. Just like me.

What if. . . . The what ifs of my life don't stop.

11

The Road to Freedom

The Course of the Disorder

Many of our patients report having had symptoms during childhood or throughout their lives, but they were insignificant or tolerable. Only in looking back do they become aware of the various different behaviors they exhibited compared to others. Perhaps they were seen as more concerned with cleanliness or generally more worried than other children. Rosemary, for instance, reported changing her dress three or four times a day because she could not tolerate dirt on it. Tom would withdraw into his room and obsess about all the kids who liked him and all those who didn't. Ann always recited a certain phrase to get a good grade, to get the date she wanted, to have a sunny day, and so on.

Most often the disorder becomes obvious during late adolescence or in the early twenties. It was only when their symptoms seriously interfered with their functioning during their early twenties that these patients sought treatment.

Usually people seek treatment when a problem gets out of hand or becomes too painful to handle. In the words of one of my professors, "People seek help when the pain of the problem becomes greater than the pain of treatment." There are people with mild forms of OCD who are never treated because they can cope with their symptoms. They are probably in the minority, though, since the course of the illness waxes and wanes with progressive worsening. Patients are often fooled by the periodic lessening of the symptoms. Symptoms may lessen for a while, but usually they increase again and, in the long run, get worse. The patient becomes frightened of more and more things and it takes him or her longer and longer to fight them. As a result of the increased urge, the intensity of the fear also increases. The sooner the patient goes for treatment, the easier and quicker it is to overcome the obsessions and compulsions.

Success or Failure in Treatment

If the proper treatment is administered and the individual follows the directions of the therapist, success is likely for the majority of patients. Of course, this assumes the correct treatment approach is used. The question of just what is the proper treatment will be addressed later. A common misconception is that the severity of the symptoms and the chronicity of the problem (how long the patient has had the disorder) are the most important factors in determining ultimate success or failure in treatment. While it may take longer to treat a patient with more severe or chronic obsessions or compulsions, it is not the only or most significant indicator of prognosis.

Severity is not always related to the duration of the problem. Sometimes, a patient who has suffered for one year may have the same severity of symptoms as a patient who has suffered twenty-two years. Usually, however, the longer a patient has had OCD, the more severe are the symptoms. Severity is judged primarily by how much symptoms interfere with the individual's daily functioning.

Factors Modifying Treatment Outcome

Whenever we have an illness, we want to know if we will improve, how long will it take, how much will we improve, and whether the illness will come back. These are natural questions. Your doctor may not always know the answers, but they are worth asking. Experience shows that some factors influence the answers to these questions. The doctor has to get to know you a little in order to assess you and then give his or her professional judgment. We have listed and then explained some factors that we believe are important in determining successful treatment. Of course, you are unique, and the presence of any one of these variables does not mean that your chances of improvement are necessarily much poorer than someone else's. Here are some factors to consider:

Overvalue ideation

Lack of motivation

Secondary gains

Personality factors

Lack of support systems

General family disturbance

Other concomitant psychiatric disorders

Prior level of functioning

Other immediate family members with OCD

Procrastination

Overvalue Ideation. Overvalue ideation refers to the strength of one's belief in the cognitions/thoughts related to the obsessions and compulsions. The stronger one's belief in the reality basis of one's fear, the more difficult it is to treat the compulsion. The weaker the strength of one's belief in the fear's being real, the better are the chances of success. While patients with OCD doubt whether their fears will come true or not, some tend to doubt it less than others. Overvalue ideators believe that the disastrous consequences of not engaging in the compulsion are more likely to occur than not. We don't know why some patients have overvalue ideation while others do not.

Randi, twenty-five years of age, feared asbestos, radiation, and AIDS. Her fears were so pervasive that she couldn't go into any grocery or department store. She was also frightened of certain relatives, and she forbade her parents from having them over. She couldn't go to various cities if she read something frightening about them, and she declined an excellent job offer because it was in a "gay" district. She indicated she desperately wanted help, yet she seemed unable to follow through with her assignments. We would expose her to a grocery store that she feared, and she would be happy to be able to purchase an item. Two weeks later, she couldn't go back because something else about the store frightened her. For example, one day Randi might be frightened because the cashier looked "sickly" and might have AIDS. Another day she would see a truck in front of the store that looked like those carrying toxic material. A third time a paint spill might scare her, and so forth.

We continued flooding (exposure) exercises and used cognitive therapy and medication, with minimal improvement compared to the effort exerted. Randi believed in her fears very strongly. She had doubts about their reality, yet each time she would think that one particular event was different from another. She believed that her evaluation of the situation had more validity than that of the therapist, her parents, or the many others who were shopping in the stores she avoided. It was extremely difficult to change her thinking.

Randi is considered to be an overvalue ideator. Patients who tend to believe in their fears more than they believe they are ridiculous are classified as overvalue ideators. If you have overvalue ideation, your success in treatment will depend upon your ability and your therapist's ability to change your belief in the reality of your fears. Overvalue ideation is a good outcome predictor. The less the patient believes in the reality of his or her fears, the more likely he or she is to succeed with drug or behavioral therapy.

Lack of Motivation. No one wants to have OCD and suffer its consequences. Yet not every patient will devote the same amount of effort to fight back symptoms and follow treatment. A patient needs motivation—a drive, an idea, or a need that incites a person to take action. Some people are more motivated to change certain aspects of their lives and less motivated to change others. One's motivation to study, work, or obtain desires is dependent upon many factors. The motivation level of a patient can be somewhat assessed by

compliance with suggestions the therapist makes

coming to therapy sessions

following treatment consistently

pushing oneself to the limit

asking others for help in resisting compulsions

We have seen patients who tell us they are highly motivated to change and overcome their obsessions and compulsions, yet they resist every form of treatment offered to them. This may partly reflect their anxiety about taking medication or their fear about experiencing anxiety during behavioral treatment. But we are always suspicious when a patient resists every option offered to him or her, for example, if a patient has a fear of taking medication and he or she is offered behavioral treatment. Or if the patient expresses fear about engaging in behavioral therapy, we might offer a nonthreatening approach allowing exposure to his or her fears in a very gradual manner. The patient then brings up another obstacle, such as a lack of transportation to come for treatment, and we begin to wonder about his or her motivation level.

We often push patients in the hope they will recognize how they put one obstacle after another in their way to improvement. We have even had patients who said, "This is me, and if you give me a medication that will take away these symptoms or take away my depression, which is reality based, then you are really taking away my identity, and therefore I don't want your treatment." Others don't want to take medication not because they are afraid of side effects, but because if they improve, it would not have been done naturally (on their own initiative).

When confronted with the fact that they originally came seeking help because they were uncomfortable with their symptoms, they continue to persist in the belief that it is dangerous to change who they are. When we find ourselves offering a million and one different ways for patients to improve and get the feeling that we are more vested in their recovery than they, then we become suspicious about their level of motivation. We are by no means suggesting that all patients who don't improve lack motivation. But it is a factor to consider.

Secondary Gains. A concept related to lack of motivation is secondary gains in having OCD. Although we don't commonly observe this factor, it deserves to be mentioned, since it is evident in some patients. Sometimes the patient and the family are unaware that having the problem enables the individual and/or the family to accrue benefits that they couldn't obtain otherwise. For example, having OCD may prevent one from assuming certain responsibilities or fulfilling expectations required in a family setting and in society.

In order for some families to function as a unit, one member must be identified as the sick one. The family unit is thus preserved when members converge on one problem and focus their attention on that one individual, thereby distracting themselves from other family problems.

Some people have a need to help others, so they remain in relationships where they are needed by the other dependent individual — "the patient." Society perceives them as martyrs or benevolent people, others may pity them, or they may receive a lot of praise or rewards coping with a sick child or spouse. If the "patient" improves, then the other person's primary role within the relationship will have to change. In order to prevent role changes, he or she has an interest in keeping the patient sick. The "patient" perceives this demand and plays the role in order to maintain the relationship because of fear of being alone, fear of not being loved, fear of change in economic status, and so forth.

A mother and son lived in a two-bedroom stucco house. She was in her late fifties, and her son John was twenty-seven years old. "Well, Doctor, here is my baby, what can you do for him?" she asked. John had a severe case of OCD. He had to quit college because he spent many hours obsessing and ritualizing. I put him on medication. The symptoms were so severe, we knew he wouldn't follow a behavioral approach. "John is my life, Doctor," said the mother. "I take care of him twenty-four hours a day. I can't go on any longer like this. Please help us both."

Three months later, we observed substantial improvement. John was able to perform household chores and leave the house to tend their garden and to shop. He felt good. The mother informed me that the treatment wasn't good and that she was disappointed. She hadn't planned on spending all her money and time on treatment. Although he had been ill since childhood, she thought three months of therapy was enough. We suggested family therapy. Eventually the truth surfaced. The mother admitted that if John improved and got a job, he would leave her. Her life would no longer have meaning.

Rose was a forty-two-year-old college graduate who was poorly groomed, weighed about 180 pounds, and had no children. Her husband cooked, cleaned the house, and did all the shopping. They had sexual intercourse only in even months on the third Sunday at 3:00 P.M. "It is a matter of superstition," said the husband in trying to explain his wife's behavior. Rose stayed in bed until late morning, washed for one hour, and ate breakfast on a couch while watching television.

She had been ill since age twenty. It began with obsessions and compulsions that lasted for about two years, then went away. One of her obsessions had been the fear of killing her children if she ever had any. Therefore, when Rose married, she and her husband decided not to have children. She had met her husband during a period free of OCD. She married at the age of twenty-five, and within six months, her symptoms had returned.

Her husband was authoritarian, a doer, a caring person who was sincerely in love. He seemed to be more of a father figure. Did he object to taking care of everything—making a living and doing housework? Not at all. He was proud of his achievements and good income. "I am a husband and a wife, two in one," he used to say. Because of his wife's illness, they did not socialize.

We outlined a treatment program. Rose was reluctant to follow it. Nevertheless, she started therapy, but after two visits she canceled appointments for blood work and psychologial testing. She decided to discontinue therapy, so we called her. "I enjoy being in the house, I love eating, and washing makes me clean. I am addicted to my obsessions, and life out there is miserable. Let my husband face the world," she said and then hung up.

Personality Factors. Each patient is a unique individual. Therefore, the obsessive-compulsive symptoms of each patient will be manifested differently. In addition, the predominant personality of the patient is very important in determining how well and to what extent he or she will respond to different treatment approaches. Over the many years of working with obsessive-compulsive patients, we noticed similar symptoms in diverse types of people. We noticed that some patients improved more rapidly than others regardless of their similar symptomatology. In our experience, patients who have histrionic, dependent, or borderline personalities are poor responders to both drug and behavioral treatment.

A histrionic person constantly seeks reassurance and approval, expresses emotions inappropriately, must be the center of attention, is overly concerned with his or her looks, and exhibits temper tantrums.

The dependent person is usually unable to make everyday decisions without excessive reassurance, agrees with others just to avoid rejection, has difficulty initiating projects, acts submissively, feels uncomfortable alone, feels devastated when close relationships end, and is preoccupied with abandonment.

The borderline personality demonstrates unstable intense interpersonal relationships fluctuating between overidealization and devaluation; marked shifts in mood usually lasting a few hours and rarely more than a few days; inappropriate intense anger or lack of control of anger; desperate efforts to avoid abandonment; attempts to split people apart; persistent identity disturbance; feelings of emptiness and boredom; suicidal thoughts; self-mutilating behavior; and impulsiveness. Of course, a given patient may show most but not necessarily all of the symptoms.

Lack of Support Systems. As with any disorder, patients who are surrounded by friends and family members who are understanding, empathic, and helpful yet not enabling have a better chance to recover. It is important to remember that compassion and empathy are not sufficient, however. Support refers to emotional and economic, as well as physical, assistance. Physical assistance refers to providing logistical services for patients, such as offering a ride to sessions, baby-sitting for their children, taking care of certain tasks, and so forth. Treatment is different for a patient who is alone, divorced, or physically ill, compared to a patient who has a good marriage and well-balanced parents and is physically healthy. Patients who are burdened with economic problems cannot put all their effort and concentration into their treatment, and this is understandable. Therefore, the patient's environment is an important variable that influences treatment outcome.

Family Disturbance. Patients who come from disturbed families will not have the support system that treatment requires. In addition, these patients may have to assume other family members' responsibilities, in addition to their own, during the acute period of their illness. Patients may not be able to handle both responsibilities simultaneously.

When we talk about family disturbance we are referring to families where anger, physical aggression, hostility, anxiety, depression, and other psychiatric problems may exist. In addition, a family member's incapacitating physical illness may distract attention from the OCD patient. Family members may have an unknowing need to keep the patient ill and send mixed messages about their devotion to the patient. Sometimes there is an inappropriate family hierarchy structure, where the children run the household.

The best way to deal with these problems is to refer the entire family to family therapy and support groups and/or to take the patient out of the disturbing environment and treat him or her alone. If possible, we recommend a halfway house, an apartment alone or with someone else, even another patient, or living with relatives or friends of the family who have a healthy family constellation. When possible, we try to create a new support system for patients by introducing them to other patients and/or helping them to become independent enough to function on their own, seek new friends, and create a new family for themselves.

Other Concomitant Psychiatric Disorders. Patients, in addition to having OCD, may have other medical and/or emotional problems that may interfere with the overall prognosis of their obsessions and compulsions. Patients who suffer from a major depression may not have the energy, motivation, and ability to combat and resist their compulsions. Patients who suffer from agoraphobia or panic disorder may have difficulty coming to treatment. Having a second psychiatric disorder may require treatment for both conditions, which may hinder the time given to the treatment of one over the other.

Some of the concomitant disorders are associated with OCD, and others are not. For example, a patient may suffer equally from OCD or have a substantial number of obsessive-compulsive symptoms, as well as an associated disorder (such as an eating disorder or Gilles de la Tourette's syndrome) or other psychiatric problems (such as depression, anxiety, or schizophrenia). It is confusing for both the patient and the therapist to determine which illness should be addressed first. Often the interference of the symptoms of the other psychiatric disorder requires that the therapist redirect treatment. This inconsistent treatment of OCD hinders habituation and thereby the overall treatment response.

Prior Level of Functioning. One day while reviewing the charts of some of our patients, we noticed that those who had been more successful in our behavioral and/or drug programs had functioned quite well before developing OCD. Since we routinely ask about our patients' level of functioning in school, work, leisure and daily routine activities, and interpersonal relationships, including sexual relations prior to their illness, it was not difficult for us to see how important prior level of functioning is in predicting treatment outcome.

Patients who are well adjusted and function well in most of these areas tend to improve sooner and return to a desirable level of functioning with greater ease than those who attained a minimal level of functioning prior to the onset of the disorder. Patients who have had difficulty completing school or going to work, who seemed to always have had difficulty relating to others or formulating and maintaining friendships, or who have been sexually and socially inhibited seem to have a poorer prognosis for recovery.

We have seen over and over again that the prior level of functioning is a predictor of future functioning and also a predictor of the ease with which patients can reduce OCD symptoms. It's understandable that patients with impaired functioning prior to developing OCD must be taught many skills after recovering from OCD. They might go to rehabilitation programs or social skills training groups. But it is difficult to explain why these same patients have more difficulty overcoming their OCD in the first place. Is it that patients who are reasonably well adjusted already have certain skills that helped them attain the moderate level of functioning before and that are now necessary to combat symptoms? This certainly seems to be the case.

Other Immediate Family Members with OCD. The presence of OCD in other family members makes treatment more difficult. This is more noticeable if these relatives are living with the patient and/or are greatly involved in his or her life.

The norms of cleanliness and organization may be very different in these families compared to the general population. The same holds true for their assessment of danger. Rather than decreasing the symptoms of the patients, they may be unwittingly increasing or maintaining the undesirable behaviors.

I remember once working with a patient who was unsure whether any member of his immediate family had OCD. After several visits to the house to conduct behavior therapy, there wasn't a doubt in my mind. The house was impeccably clean; not a single object was out of place. During one visit, while concentrating intensely on our exposure exercise and drinking coffee, we left coffee stains on the kitchen counter. While the stain could have been easily wiped off, the patient's wife, upon arriving home, became very anxious and went on a cleaning spree. After several such encounters, I began to wash off the counter and leave everything organized before leaving. Finally I realized what I was doing. It was very easy to see why my patient found it difficult to resist his own compulsions while his wife was also compulsive.

Procrastination. While procrastination seems to be an obvious modifying factor of treatment outcome, it is usually ignored. All of us, at one point or another, have put off doing things and made up excuses why it would be better to do them tomorrow. Of course, tomorrow never comes. There's always one more excuse. But when starting treatment, one cannot procrastinate, since the symptoms could get progressively worse. The longer one puts off fighting the disorder, the more severe the symptoms may get.

We have had patients come in for consultations and make appointments for future sessions and then cancel them. They come back a year or more later and indicate that they postponed treatment because they were frightened, thought the disorder would improve by itself, or thought if they waited long enough a magical cure would be discovered. Sometimes patients fool themselves by putting off treatment until they move, go on vacation, or see their children graduate, thinking it would be better to start therapy when they are "more settled." Unfortunately, treatment may be more difficult in the future. Of course, there are probably many patients who procrastinate sufficiently never to receive treatment.

What are the chances of a cure? At the present time, there is no complete cure for OCD. Treatment is geared to reduce or suppress symptoms. The disorder may be likened to alcoholism. If one is an alcoholic, one is always an alcoholic. The minute one gives in to the desire to drink after abstaining, the problem returns. Over a period of abstinence, however, it gets easier and easier to resist the urge to drink. Alcoholics Anonymous (AA) initially teaches individuals to stay away from situations that may lead to drinking behavior. Eventually, alcoholics, over a period of time, may be able to go into a bar and not drink. But if they give in to the urge to drink, then the need to drink may come right back. The desire to drink lessens with time, however, so even in the presence of liquor the alcoholic can abstain. A similar situation exists for patients with OCD. Once they can resist the compulsion, the urge decreases. If at any point the patient gives in to the compulsion, the whole disorder may reappear. For this reason, we state there is no cure. The same applies to obsessions.

Usually obsessions that are related to compulsions disappear shortly after the compulsive behavior ceases. Obsessions unrelated to compulsions are more resistant to treatment. Obsessions may be reduced with medication. Also, behavior therapy is effective with obsessions that are superstitious or morbid or have disastrous consequences attached to them. While the obsession may never come back, there are no guarantees that it won't. But the symptoms never return to the same degree of severity and can be easily treated by reapplying the same treatment techniques. Occasional booster sessions may be needed or, periodically, medications may have to be resumed.

Is there spontaneous remission? The answer is *no.* While for some disorders, such as depression, the symptoms may just go away on their own, this is not true for OCD. The symptoms just get worse. They may lessen at times, but never disappear. Don't count on spontaneous recovery.

Is there symptom substitution? Psychoanalysts have expressed concern over symptom substitution for some time. Symptom substitution refers to the belief that unless the underlying causes of OCD are discovered and treated, it will not suffice to control symptoms with behavior therapy. In place of obsessions and compulsions, the patient will substitute other symptoms. In this assumption lies the theory that OCD is caused by unresolved conflicts, primarily during toilet training, and that insight will lead to cure. Based on this theory, psychoanalysts believe that if the basis for the obsessions and compulsions that rests in unresolved childhood conflicts is not treated, other fears will be substituted for the OCD.

We do not believe there are hidden, unknown underlying causes to the disorder. Follow-up studies conducted over several years have all demonstrated that symptom substitution does not occur. Another problem or disorder is not substituted in place of the OCD. That is not to say that obsessions or compulsions may not change; in fact, one obsession or compulsion may be replaced by another during the course of treatment. However, once the treatment is completed, another problem does not take the place of OCD.

DEALING WITH RELAPSE

You are probably wondering whether you will relapse. In order to answer this question, it must be assumed that you have been successfully treated. Obviously, you cannot relapse if you haven't reduced or eliminated your obsessive-compulsive symptoms. As with any disorder, relapse is contingent upon improvement. Relapse may be only temporary and recovery rather quick, if certain precautions are taken. As stated before, OCD is a chronic condition, meaning that you must be monitored and certain precautions must be taken to prevent relapse.

Sometimes relapse occurs during active intensive treatment. This setback usually lasts only a couple of days until the patient resumes resisting the urges. If stress causes the relapse, one should work toward stress control. It's important for patients and families not to become anxious over these periodic setbacks and to push forward. To make a catastrophe of these events leads to further anxiety, which, in turn, may increase symptoms.

It is better to expect a relapse and be prepared for it. If you don't immediately combat the symptoms during the relapse, a full-blown recurrence of the disorder is possible. There is no need to panic, even if this happens. Treatment can be reimplemented, and response will be easier and quicker than the first time around. It is imperative to restart treatment immediately.

The main causes of relapse are these:

Feeling out of control

Anxiety

Stress

Fatigue

Partial improvement

Speeding up rituals and cautious looking

Long-standing habits

Overdependency on therapist guidance

Medication withdrawal

Feeling Out of Control. Originally, compulsions may have been performed to obtain an illusion of control over the environment. Whether this was the impetus or not, the patient usually has a sense of loss of control when the symptoms get out of hand. Once the symptoms decrease or are eliminated, the patient usually feels in control again. This is a dangerous junction. While we repeatedly tell patients to be aware of this crossroad and to realize they are never fully in control of the symptoms, most relapses occur at this point. No matter how much we warn patients, they don't comprehend the seriousness of the warning. They feel in control, on top of the world, and they see no harm in giving in to one urge. One urge may lead to two or three urges, and before the patient knows it, the problem snowballs. It doesn't mean the patient always needs to be compulsive. The longer the abstinence from compulsions, the less the urge, and the easier to resist. Nevertheless, be it a month, six months, or five years after terminating treatment, an urge may be experienced, and at this point the patient's sense of control will be tested. All we can say is *do not give in.*

Anxiety. While we can go into a whole discourse on what is anxiety, suffice to say that the word *anxiety,* as used here, refers to specific or unspecific fear. As mentioned before, anxiety over a temporary setback during active treatment may lead to a vicious cycle: setback – anxiety – setback – anxiety and so on, until a full-blown relapse occurs. It is important to be prepared for temporary setbacks and to forge ahead in resisting compulsions. Enlisting the help of others at this point is very important. One or two victories over the symptoms will lead the patient back on the road to full recovery.

Anxiety may also occur over other events at any point in the patient's life. Anxiety is not a sure bet for relapse; but it can occur if the patient's urge to give in to a compulsion increases during the anxious period, creating a *snowballing effect.*

Anxiety may be experienced during times of conflict and/or in phobic situations. After treating the obsessions and compulsions, it is important to address secondary problems. For example, patients who have difficulty interacting with others, who are basically nonassertive and dependent on others, and who lack problem-solving skills are more apt to experience anxiety in a variety of situations. The patient has to be treated in an integral manner, whereby phobias, marital/family conflicts, assertion problems, and the like must be focused upon during treatment. An overall emphasis on anxiety reduction must be present. This is not to suggest that anxiety reduction or the treatment of secondary problems be the focus of treatment. It is important to directly treat the obsessions and compulsions via appropriate medication and/or behavior therapy.

Stress. Stress is related to anxiety, although the patient may not actually experience specific or unspecific fear. In fact, the person under stress may not even know it.

Following are some of the symptoms of stress:

Fatigue	Difficulty thinking
Forgetfulness	Perspiration
Poor concentration	Cold hands and feet
Limited attention span	Muscular tension
Mixing up words	Twitching

Tics	Hypoactivity
Nausea	Irritability
Hyperactivity	Insomnia

Many life events are considered stressful for most people. The Social Readjustment Rating Scale, found in appendix A, enables anyone to determine his or her current stress level. Death of a loved one, change in job, marriage, divorce, birth, and relocation are all possible stressful events. How an individual reacts to these events is important, rather than the event itself. What is stressful for one may not be for another. Unlike anxiety, though, stress may not be as easily identifiable. Once again, if the urge returns or its intensity increases, it is necessary to resist.

Fatigue. Fatigue may occur for myriad reasons. Some causes of fatigue follow:

Stress

Insomnia

Side effect of medication

Worry

Overwork

Physical illness

Menstruation

Stress and lack of sleep are the most common causes of fatigue. Insomnia must be corrected. It's important to sleep the same number of hours to which you are usually accustomed in order to avoid fatigue. Sometimes fatigue is a side effect of medication, which can be corrected if brought to the physician's attention. Other times, it may be caused by worry. Realize that worrying has never solved problems; on the contrary, it usually leads to further problems.

Fatigue may also be caused by overworking. Workaholism, in or outside the house, will eventually wear you out. While it is good to keep busy, the extreme is unhealthy. Moderation in everything is best. Fatigue may also occur as a result of a physical illness, even a mild cold. Whatever the reason, it is a time when the patient's urge to give in to a compulsion may recur or an obsession may reappear. Prevention is always the best mode of handling possible mental or physical illness, but when not feasible, the patient must resort to previously successful treatment methods.

Partial Improvement. No matter how much we insist that patients try to fight all their obsessions and compulsions, we inevitably have patients who are satisfied with partial improvement. This is understandable because it takes a lot of effort to resist compulsions, and if a patient can function relatively well after years of minimal functioning, he or she is happy.

One woman had had OCD for twenty-five years without a day's relent. She was literally living on a couch in one room of her house; she also kept all her belongings on that couch. She was utterly frightened every time she had to use the bathroom or eat, since it meant having contact with contaminated objects. Slowly, with therapy, she overcame many of her fears, but there were certain places she couldn't go and some objects she couldn't touch. We wanted her to overcome these few remaining fears, but she was satisfied with her partial improvement. She indicated that she had no interest in going to those places—would never go even if she could—and therefore she saw no reason to work on them. We explained that partial improvement means that remnants of irrational thinking may predominate in all areas at any time.

Partial improvement may be the patient's choice, as in the example above, or a function of the extreme anxiety attached to certain obsessions and compulsions and the patient's inability to fight it. Regardless of the reason, the chances of relapse are greater with partial improvement than with complete improvement. The patient's thought process must change completely, and he or she should make an effort to overcome every single symptom. There is no need for partial improvement. If thoughts and behaviors are changeable in some areas, then they are changeable in all.

Speeding Up Rituals and Cautious Looking. Some patients erroneously believe that the interference of their symptoms in their lives, rather than the symptoms themselves, is important. Therefore, they direct their energies toward lessening the interference rather than eliminating the obsessions and compulsions. Of course, it is the therapist's responsibility to indicate that, unless the symptoms are eliminated, the seeds for relapse lie dormant. Gradually, the duration, intensity, and frequency of the symptoms may increase and begin to interfere in the patient's daily functioning. But the therapist and family members may be unaware that the symptoms are still present, and the patient may not realize the importance of reporting them.

Many times we ask patients to reduce their shower time to ten minutes. In fact, we may take such precautions as having them timed, having someone pull them out of the shower, and/or centrally turning off the water. Eventually, most patients comply. After treating many patients, we began to question *how* they showered in ten minutes. To our surprise, they would describe the same or slightly modified rituals as before, but speeded up. In other words, they would still thoroughly soap every part of the body, making sure not to miss a part, then wash the hair and upper torso, then clean the washcloth until "sterilized," and then wash the genital area and legs. Instead of taking forty-five minutes, the shower now takes ten minutes. Patients are content because they have more time; no longer are they late for appointments or a nuisance to other family members who may want to use the bathroom. Everyone is happy, including the therapist, who may not have asked about speeding up.

The process of speeding up may occur in any form of compulsion and is not restricted to washing. One can speed up magical thinking rituals, counting, checking a certain number of times, and touching objects or parts of one's body. Speeding up reduces the interference of the obsessions and compulsions, but the thoughts and fears attached to the compulsions remain relatively untouched.

Similar in concept to speeding up is *cautious looking*. One patient who checked light switches, appliances, doors, and faucets several times before going to bed became a "cautious looker" with our treatment. In other words, rather than checking several times, the patient looked arduously at various objects to make sure they were locked, closed, turned off, or unplugged. By no means was this our goal, but she had found a new way to approach an old problem. Cautious looking occurs when a patient is vigilant, looks attentively, and concentrates hard on what he or she is doing. The vigilance or cautious looking takes the place of a whole investigative process that might have taken place prior to treatment. Of course, as in the case of speeding up, cautious looking indicates that the thoughts, fears, and general approach to life events have not been changed much. There must be a complete modification of these processes if there is to be a genuine improvement and reduction in the probability of relapse.

Long-standing Habits. Every one of us has a tendency to return to old habits, even when we don't want to. They are familiar, easy to carry out, almost automatic, and well established. Yet we don't see many OCD patients who resort to compulsions just out of habit. It deserves to be mentioned, though, for the few who may relapse unknowingly. When a patient thinks, "I don't know why I just did that. I didn't have to," he or she may be returning to old habits. The compulsive behavior occurs in the absence of an urge to perform the compulsion. For example, patients may find themselves avoiding a piece of furniture they have used since treatment but did not use for ten years previously. Or they may find themselves washing their hands in between every different food item while preparing dinner, although they had not done this since their treatment.

How does one account for the return of old habits? Environmental cues that previously elicited compulsions have the power to evoke the same response spontaneously and periodically. It may be related to spontaneous recall from memory and learned behavioral responses. This is unrelated to anxiety, which may heighten the connection between certain environmental cues and obsessive-compulsive behavior. If the obsessive-compulsive behavior is repeated over time because of long-standing habits, the urge, thoughts, and feelings associated with the behavior may return, and a full-blown relapse may occur.

Overdependency on Therapist Guidance. Initially, patients depend on the therapist to learn methods of controlling their obsessions and compulsions. They rely on the therapist's judgment of what is appropriate and what is not, what is dangerous and what is not. Eventually they need to learn to make those assessments on their own.

Some patients' trust is so unyielding that they may not even experience much anxiety during treatment if the therapist is present. While this is fine, and patients can still improve, it is important to teach patients to trust themselves and to make decisions. The inability to make decisions and doubting are common problems in obsessive-compulsives. This is why they often seek the reassurance of others and of their therapist. Patients depend on others. In the long run, a strong dependency is unhealthy because in the absence of the therapist, the patient may not continue to practice exposure and response prevention.

We have seen patients relapse and return for further treatment. When we asked why they didn't immediately implement the methods they had learned, they didn't know. It was as if they were waiting for some authority to tell them what to do. During these booster sessions, they had to be told what to do step by step, as if they had never had treatment. If the patient and the therapist are aware of the dependency, then certain precautions may be taken against it. It may not be evident, however, in some patients who appear to be independent, comply with homework assignments, and do not ask for reassurance. It only becomes evident if the urge resurfaces and the patient gives in and a snowballing effect occurs. Sometimes the dependency is evident when a patient doubts or expresses concern over a decision and begins to doubt himself or herself.

To discourage overdependency we encourage patients to practice exposure and response prevention gradually on their own. While we initially practice some exercises with patients, we slowly pull back and ask them to do it on their own.

Medication Withdrawal. A patient's response to medication withdrawal is not easily determined. It is quite difficult to predict whether a patient will relapse or not following discontinuation of drug therapy. There are many factors to consider in predicting the probability of relapse after medication withdrawal. Naturally, this prediction is not 100 percent accurate; therefore, one is limited in predicting treatment outcome. Note these factors to consider before drug withdrawal:

Whether the patient has undergone behavior therapy

Medication used

Dosage

Length of use

Side effects

Toxic effects

Patient's response to medication

What effect medication had in improving the patient's condition

Presence or absence of important life events or stressors currently in the patient's life

Treatment duration

Whether the patient has been taught other ways to cope with anxiety, depression, obsessions, and compulsions

Obviously, if the medication seriously affects the health of the patient, the drug has to be withdrawn. Because other drugs may not have the same side effect, it may be justifiable to switch to a new medication.

Depending on the drug and the answer to the questions, the relapse rate may vary. Even well-researched drugs have yielded different relapse rates, anywhere from 33 to 99 percent, depending on the particular investigation. Everyone is unique, and therefore each response to treatment, as well as each relapse rate, differs. Some research indicates that those patients who receive appropriate behavioral treatment in addition to medication have less chance of relapse than those who receive only medication. This makes sense, since there is no cure for the disorder, and behavior therapy teaches the patient how to control symptoms.

PREVENTING RELAPSE

We discussed many possible reasons for relapse. Of course, some things we don't have much control over, and other things we do. *Snowballing effect* was a term we used repeatedly to explain how relapse occurs, regardless of the preceding circumstances. If patients can prevent themselves from engaging in the obsessions or compulsions at all times, then relapse will not occur. That's the only sure way to prevent relapse. Otherwise, if a patient gives in and the snowballing effect takes place, then relapse will occur. The extent of the relapse will vary according to when the patient stops the compulsions. If a patient appears unable to stop, then friends or family members should assist him or her, and therapy should be resumed. As stated before, OCD is a chronic condition and needs to be kept in check at all times.

Here are some suggestions on how to keep your OCD in check.

Build follow-up sessions into treatment

Deal with all the problems

Know under what conditions relapse may occur

Reduce overall stress

Build a new future

Allow some family and friends to be involved

Build Follow-up Sessions into Treatment. Much of the research indicates that those patients who continue in treatment for one or two years after successful treatment are less likely to relapse. Further sessions to follow up the patient allow for consolidation of gains made during treatment. During this time, the therapist may become aware of early signs of relapse and help prevent it. The sessions may be used to work on other problem areas.

Deal with All the Problems. Some patients are satisfied with partial improvement. When compared to the symptoms they had at the time they entered treatment, they perceive a 100 percent change. But no matter how much a person changes, if it isn't complete, the chances of relapse are greater than if they had dealt with all aspects of the disorder. There must be an overall change in cognitions for treatment to be very effective.

Also, to reduce stress and anxiety unrelated to OCD, other problem areas should be explored. New methods of coping should be learned. Many patients with OCD find their lives shattered, even after successful treatment. It is important to reconstruct patients' lives.

Know under What Conditions Relapse May Occur. It is important for the patient, as well as family members, to become acquainted with the conditions under which relapse occurs. With knowledge, they can be alerted to precipitating factors and can take control of the situation before snowballing occurs. Also, one can avoid putting himself or herself in a position where the chances of relapse are greater. In this chapter, we have dicussed what to look for and avoid.

Reduce Overall Stress. Repeatedly, we have emphasized to our patients the importance of reducing stress, anxiety, and fatigue in their lives. Relaxing, meditating, managing time appropriately, using coping skills, developing desirable and logical thoughts, and being assertive are all ways of reducing stress. If such skills are lacking, then they should be taught by the therapist and learned by the patient.

Build a New Future. It is important for all of us to have things to look forward to and to enjoy living. For most patients, obsessions and compulsions dominate their lives and the joy of living dies down. Even if they aren't depressed, life is a struggle, and daily living is an effort. Lives are destroyed. Once the disorder is treated, patients sometimes don't know how to direct their lives. It's like starting all over again and having a million and one options but not knowing which one to choose. A new future must be built in order to move away from unpleasant past associations and habits.

Allow Some Family and Friends to Be Involved. Patients should allow some people into their secretive world of OCD. Disclosing some of their fears can decrease their chances of relapse for many reasons. First, patients are embarrassed to perform rituals or reluctant to ask for reassurance when they know the people around them will prevent them from giving in to these urges. In addition, friends or family may even be able to serve as co-therapists and expose patients to their fears knowingly and prevent them from ritualizing. Second, people close to the patient will be alert to subtle signs of the reoccurrence of symptoms. Thus, they can bring it to the attention of the patient, who may remain unaware. Third, family and friends may be supportive and alleviate the feelings of isolation and loneliness.

I am alone on this earth. No one else exists.

I wash my hands to prevent a catastrophe. If I don't, my dad might die.

It takes me the whole day in one single department store to buy a shirt. I keep walking back and forth among the aisles. Sometimes security has asked me to leave the store. Recently I have been banned from two stores.

Is it I in the mirror, or is it someone else? And yesterday? And a week ago? How about now? Or tomorrow?

Epilogue: 100 Questions

1. *What is OCD?*   OCD is an illness characterized by persistent, intrusive, useless thoughts, accompanied by the urge to perform repetitive and bizarre-seeming acts.

2. *How common is obsessive-compulsive disorder?*   Obsessive-compulsive disorder appears to affect between 3 percent and 5 percent of the general population.

3. *What do I need?*   OCD sufferers need security, certainty, to be in control, to preserve, and to repeat.

4. *What does OCD mean to me?*

Slavery

Pain

Fear

To be dead, yet alive

Transient stage

My own self

An act

A biochemical imbalance

Permanent state

A mistake (why me?)

A punishment

To be possessed

5. *What is dysmorphophobia?* Dysmorphophobia, or Body Dysmorphic Disorder (BDD), is a belief that one's face or body is defective, when to others the individual appears normal. The person is usually concerned with his or her nose, jaw, wrinkles, scars, or body weight. The person with BDD usually remains isolated from others.

6. *Is OCD nonsensical?* Most of the OCD activities are nonsensical, for example, double-checking or handwashing unnecessarily.

7. *Do I need to be in control?* Patients suffering from OCD need to be in control of people, events, fate, and even death.

8. *What will happen if I give up my need to be in control?* You will be quite frightened unless you learn how to cope with not being in control. Your sense of being in control, however, is probably false.

9. *Should I give up all control?* Find out what is sensible to control, and discard what is not.

10. *Isn't it easier to say it than to do it?* Yes, but you ought to start somewhere.

11. *Are patients suffering from OCD self-centered?* Most patients are self-centered. They spend all their time discussing their illness. Everything revolves around them, because their problems interfere with their normal lives. They can't help but think about their illness since it usually occupies a large portion of their day and causes great distress.

12. *Does self-centeredness affect social relationships?* It does. Who wants to listen to someone else's problems all day long? Life is a two-way street. One gives to receive, and vice versa.

13. *Why can't I make up my mind on anything?* Because doubting is one of the serious OCD symptoms.

14. *Why is doubting a serious symptom?* Because it prevents you from going about your everyday life. It doesn't allow you to program your life, relate to people, work, and build up a future. You become dependent.

15. *Is doubting always a serious symptom?* Not at all. Some patients have no difficulty in deciding on school, work, or marriage, but they cannot make up their minds about everyday things, such as what to wear, what color shirt to buy, what to eat, or which television program to watch.

16. *What will happen if I keep procrastinating?* You will fail. Patients procrastinate about daily chores, work, decision making, even their treatment programs. Procrastination may jeopardize treatment outcome.

17. *Will I be able to have a family?* It depends on the severity of the illness. Marriage requires mutual love and care, and most important, a capacity for dialogue and listening as well. If you have uncontrollable symptoms, the process of interacting normally with others will be altered. Obsessions usually interfere with the process of interacting. Compulsions may keep you from seeking out a partner. If your symptoms are under control, you can marry and have children.

18. *Will I be able to have children?* The disease does not interfere with fertility or pregnancy.

19. *Will pregnancy affect my illness?* Pregnancy usually affects the mood of women already suffering from an emotional disorder. This may be seen in patients suffering from OCD as well. Postpartum depression may occur in patients with OCD.

20. *Does pregnancy cause OCD?* No, pregnancy does not cause it, but it can precipitate it. Pregnancy may exacerbate already existing symptoms. Patients who have a predisposition to OCD may first experience their symptoms during pregnancy or immediately after delivery.

21. *If I had not gotten pregnant, would I have developed OCD?* Probably. Pregnancy was a likely precipitating factor; if it wasn't, some other event would have triggered it.

22. *If I am treated, will another pregnancy produce a relapse?* Not necessarily. In fact, if you have learned how to control your symptoms with behavioral techniques, use the techniques again if you suffer a relapse during pregnancy. Just don't give in. Then the symptoms won't recur. Further pregnancies may not necessarily precipitate a reoccurrence of the symptoms.

23. *Can menstruation affect my symptoms?* Over the years, patients have reported having more urges just prior to or during their menstrual periods. For patients who suffer from premenstrual syndrome, there is a general increase in anxiety, irritability, and nervous tension for several days before menstruation. While symptoms may vary from muscle stiffness, headaches, confusion, crying, depression, burst of energy, and orderliness to excitement, there is no doubt that hormonal changes can upset well-being or stability. During the first several months of treatment, patients become alarmed at the prospect of relapse. They feel more anxious, possibly more depressed, and worst of all, they find it harder to fight compulsions. The urge to give in increases. They are sure these are the warning signals of relapse. If at this point they give in, and continue to give in, to their compulsions, then certainly partial relapse may occur. This is usually not the case, however. We point out to patients that their increased urges are attributable to premenstrual syndrome, and within a few days the symptoms will go away. We encourage them to resist and wait. Once they are convinced they can wait it out, the urges decrease.

24. *Will I be able to raise my children?* Because the illness may interfere with every aspect of life, raising your children may become a hardship. Intensity and severity of symptoms play a role in determining how much of your time you can dedicate to your children. The minimum requirements of feeding and clothing them and sending them to school are usually not affected.

25. *Will my spouse divorce me if I have OCD?* If the OCD goes untreated for several years, a gradual deterioration of the relationship will occur. It is very hard to live with someone suffering from an illness that invades all layers of life. The tension, anger, and need to depend on others eventually may exhaust your partner.

26. *How can I prevent this from occurring?* As soon as you notice that you are ill, go for help immediately. Remember, it takes the average patient about seven to ten years from the onset of illness to the time he or she seeks treatment. The sooner you seek help, the better your chances of recovery.

27. *Are there any other reasons for divorce?* Yes. When the "healthy" spouse find his or her spouse improved, the couple may decide to divorce. Some spouses feel strongly obligated to stay as long as the illness remains uncontrolled. This moral issue is no longer present once the spouse is doing well.

28. *Do I have to remain ill to keep my marriage together?* Under certain circumstances, if you are aware of the possibility of losing your spouse, you have to discuss your feelings and worries openly. Marital therapy will be quite helpful as long as you don't procrastinate, and your spouse is willing to participate.

29. *Will my illness affect my children?* It may affect your children if they are very young and you raise them primarily yourself. Some of the obsessive-compulsive behaviors that you show may be learned by your children. They may develop an obsessive-compulsive personality. About 8 percent of OCD sufferers have parents who are OCD sufferers themselves.

30. *Will I be able to make friends?* OCD is an illness that will close you in. You will be in your own world of doubts, obsessions, and compulsions. Friendship requires openness, sharing, and caring. If you are busy with your illness, it will be difficult to maintain friendships.

31. *Will I maintain friendships?* As the disorder progresses, we find that people gradually lose their friends. It is difficult even to maintain phone contact. Very often friends don't know why a separation has occurred. Patients become too frightened of their friends, too preoccupied with their obsessions or compulsions, too embarrassed to be seen if they become unkempt. They may feel envious of friends' life-style and health. If you feel comfortable with one or two friends and think they will understand, it is best to explain your disorder.

32. *Are birth abnormalities or complications related to OCD?* Very few patients had abnormal births or complications at delivery. Abnormal duration of pregnancy, such as premature or overdue birth, occurs in 27 percent of the cases, a Caesarean section is performed in 21 percent of the cases, and forceps are used in 19 percent of the cases. Birth complications are present in about 11 percent of the cases. These numbers are not different from the general population. Birth abnormalities or complications might in some cases be related to OCD, but this should be considered on an individual basis.

33. *If I have OCD, am I susceptible to having an additional emotional disorder?* We have found that 51 percent of the patients suffer from concomitant phobias.

34. *Are patients with OCD likely to be alcoholics?* This is a good question because patients suffering from OCD have so many compulsions, why not a compulsion to drink? In one of our studies, 42 percent out of 307 patients did not drink at all, 10 percent of the patients had two or more drinks a day, and 11 percent were problem drinkers. These percentages are very different when compared to the general population. For example, 86 percent of the general population drinks as compared to our findings of 48 percent within the OCD population.

35. *Are obsessive-compulsive patients likely to be drug abusers?* Obsessive-compulsive patients do not abuse drugs any more or less than the general population.

36. *What is an acute illness?* An acute illness is a disease that starts with a sudden onset and has a short duration.

37. *What is a chronic disease?* A chronic disease is a disease that may start suddenly or gradually and lasts for more than a month or so.

38. *Is OCD acute or chronic?* OCD is not an acute illness. OCD has a gradual onset and is chronic.

39. *Does OCD have peaks?* Yes. OCD has peaks mainly between the ages of twenty and forty. It seems that biological and social changes affect the illness. Male middle-age crisis and female menopause might trigger a relapse of the illness. Other events that precipitate an onset of the illness are weddings, divorces, births, deaths in the family, the loss of a job, going away to college, and retirement. Stress is an important factor.

40. *Is OCD curable?* OCD is not curable, although there are cases of complete remission without relapse. At present there is no cure. It is, however, a *treatable* illness.

41. *What is the aim of treatment for OCD?* The aim of treatment for OCD is to control the symptoms and to permit the patient to continue to lead a functional life. Functionality is the aim of treatment. Most treatments are geared to alleviate and suppress the duration, intensity, and frequency of the symptoms, as well as to restore the ability to function to the patient.

42. *Does stress aggravate OCD?* Yes, stress aggravates OCD. By controlling your stress level you will help to control the disorder.

43. *Do weather conditions affect OCD?* Weather conditions do not affect OCD. In patients who suffer from the OCD manic-depressive form, however, the beginning of spring or winter may affect the course of the disease.

44. *What is the influence of OCD on sexual intercourse?* The influence of OCD on intercourse is relative. If the person is severely obsessive, obsessions may remain present during sexual intercourse. Serious obsessive-compulsive symptoms cause depression, which decreases sexual desire. Sexual practices are also affected in those patients obsessed with sexual matters. Fear of contamination, if present, may hinder a good sexual relationship.

45. *Does the use of cocaine affect OCD?* The use of cocaine may aggravate OCD symptomatology.

46. *Does the use of LSD affect OCD?* The use of LSD may aggravate OCD symptomatology.

47. *Does the use of marijuana affect OCD?* Marijuana, by producing relaxation, helps to relieve OCD symptoms, such as anxiety, temporarily. But good-quality marijuana also causes depression and hallucinations. It is certainly not a way to control the disorder in the long run.

48. *Will masturbation alleviate my symptoms of OCD?* Masturbation, by producing relaxation, may temporarily alleviate some OCD symptoms. For those patients who masturbate compulsively, however, masturbation becomes another OCD symptom.

49. *Will OCD medication affect my sexual drive?* Yes, medication may affect your sexual drive. Loss of sexual desire, loss of orgasm, and delayed ejaculation are side effects of anti–obsessive-compulsive drugs.

50. *How do obsessions affect intercourse?* Obsessions about sexual aberrations, incest, infidelity, and homosexuality may lead to tremendous anxiety, which can prevent one from having or enjoying intercourse. Also, during intercourse, patients sometimes engage in ritualistic praying and/or neutralizing thoughts to counteract unacceptable sexual fantasies, which prevents lovemaking.

51. *How do compulsions affect intercourse?* Patients with fear of contamination are often unable to touch their partners. They may be afraid of getting or giving AIDS, herpes, or venereal diseases. Sometimes patients believe sex is dirty, or they specifically fear sperm.

52. *Will OCD affect my libido?* Yes, indeed, OCD may affect your libido, usually by decreasing it. In a very few instances, sexual desire increases. Everything turns on the obsessive nature of the illness, which quite often doesn't allow the person to have sexual intercourse or to feel sexually aroused.

53. *Can OCD affect my orgasm?* Yes, OCD may affect your orgasm, and in many instances may even produce complete anorgasmia or frigidity. Obsessions and severe anxiety that accompany the disorder are the culprits.

54. *Can OCD accelerate or delay my ejaculation?* OCD may accelerate ejaculation, depending on the amount of anxiety present. For those patients who are on tricyclic medication, a side effect of this medication may be delayed ejaculation or suppression of ejaculation altogether.

55. *Is it better to masturbate than to have sex?* This is an interesting question. We have observed that many patients suffering from OCD and agoraphobia derive more pleasure from masturbation than from sexual intercourse. This is usually the case with patients who are self-centered and/or have many sexual fears.

56. *Is OCD learned?* Yes, it can be, although only 5 percent of the mothers and 3 percent of the fathers of patients with OCD have the illness. Therefore, it doesn't seem likely that patients have picked it up from their parents.

57. *Why did I develop OCD?* No one really knows exactly why. But there are biological and psychological theories to explain why one may develop the disorder.

58. *Is it because my serotonin is low?* Serotonin is a substance (neurotransmitter) in the body. Some patients have low serotonin, but not all patients do.

59. *Can there be other biological reasons?* The fact that your serotonin level is normal doesn't mean there aren't other substances related to serotonin that are altered. Not enough research has been conducted yet. It takes a long time to discover or to put research findings into the right perspective.

60. *What are the psychological theories?* Psychoanalysts believe OCD develops from unresolved conflicts during childhood, primarily during toilet training.

61. *How did the serotonin theory develop?* It developed as a result of the evaluation and analysis of the action of anti–obsessive-compulsive drugs. These drugs work by making larger amounts of serotonin available in the brain. Therefore, it was assumed there must be a serotonin deficiency related to OCD.

62. *How did the behavioral theory develop?* It developed originally from animal studies. Fixated or stereotyped behaviors in animals that are similar to human compulsive behaviors are difficult to remove. Rats were manually guided to a previously avoided situation and prevented from carrying out a fixed response. The avoidance behavior was thereby extinguished or stopped. In 1966, this method was applied to two patients.

63. *What changes will I see with behavior therapy?* The therapist looks for changes in duration, intensity, and frequency of compulsions and obsessions. Duration refers to the amount of time spent on symptoms during the day (doing or avoiding); intensity refers to how anxious or uncomfortable one feels; and frequency is the number of times the symptom occurs. In our experience, the first change is usually seen in the reduction of the intensity, followed by a shortening of the duration, and then by a decrease in the frequency of the thoughts. The number of times the patient engages in the compulsion decreases immediately, but the frequency of the thoughts remains quite high for some time, despite the reduction in behavioral response.

64. *Is it better to avoid than to be compulsive?* There is little difference if you avoid an object, situation, or person or if you perform a compulsion because in either case you are reacting to the compulsive urge.

65. *Is it all right to postpone a ritual?* It is best to resist performing a ritual. Postponement does not lead to elimination of symptoms. It is, however, better to postpone than to give in immediately because you might change your mind later and avoid the ritual.

66. *Is suicide common among OCD patients?* No. In fact it is very uncommon. Rarely do patients with OCD commit suicide, despite their depression about their symptoms and inability to function. Yet we always become very concerned when a patient talks about suicide. Nobody should take suicidal thoughts lightly.

67. *Is homicidal behavior common?* No. Homicide is not the norm in patients with OCD.

68. *Why do I have difficulties handling mail?* Over the years, we have observed a large percentage of people who are unable to open mail. For the majority of the patients, the problem is related to fear of contamination. They don't know who touched the letter or whether that letter touched another letter from a "contaminated city or state." Once the mail is accepted, a new problem arises: where to put it and avoid contaminating other objects.

69. *How does the average person shower?* While this sounds silly, many patients with OCD forget how to shower normally. We always suggest that patients watch someone. If this is impossible, then have your therapist, family member, or friend demonstrate. Most people don't wash every part of their body or they don't necessarily start with their hair so all the contamination goes to the rest of the body, which will eventually be decontaminated. In fact, most people shower to be clean, not decontaminated.

70. *Why is my hair so important?* Many patients don't like to touch their hair. While they may allow other body parts to touch the floor or various objects, they are reluctant to expose their hair. Why the hair is sacred, we don't know. Perhaps it is because it is difficult to clean.

71. *Why are my feet so important?* Most patients will not touch their feet. They consider them very dirty. Even in the shower, they think of all the "contaminants" getting on their feet, but the prospect of washing them is almost unbearable. Patients will go to great lengths not to have the bottom of their slacks touch their feet, in order not to dirty the slacks. Perhaps because our feet touch the rug (which has all the contaminants from the soles of our shoes), they have to be isolated from the rest of the body.

72. *Am I allowed to drink?* If you have OCD, you may drink, providing you don't abuse alcohol. If you are under treatment, however, you may not do so. It has been shown that anti – obsessive-compulsive agents in combination with alcohol may produce aggressive behavior. Furthermore, alcohol may cause depression as well. Therefore, you will be better off refraining from drinking.

73. *Is OCD a neurological illness?* OCD is not a pure neurological illness, although some forms of OCD may present neurological signs. The brain controls the activity of the mind and nervous system. Therefore, it is expected that psychiatric and neurological disorders may have both neurological and psychiatric symptoms.

74. *If I suffer from OCD, will I lose my mind?* Those who suffer from OCD will never lose their minds. Patients with OCD are in touch with reality. Their sense of reality is never lost, and patients are always rational. It is different when a patient suffers from schizophrenia with OCD symptoms. In that case, one may become irrational owing to the schizophrenia. But the primary obsessive-compulsive disorder is not a form of psychosis. Reality and reason remain intact.

75. *Does OCD affect the family structure?* Yes, OCD may in some cases affect the family structure and create significant disturbance. For example, out of 67 patients interviewed, 58 percent reported family problems or family disorders.

76. *How does society see a patient suffering from OCD?* Because of the secretiveness of the symptoms, most of the time your social environment will not come in contact with the privacy of your illness. Therefore, other people won't be able to judge you. There are certain behaviors, however, that may be unacceptable, embarrassing, even punishable if discovered, and you may not want to expose yourself to ostracism. Other than that, your condition should not produce rejection; if anything, there should be more support because you are in contact with reality.

77. *Sometimes I believe that I do not think, and therefore that I do not exist.* Such thinking indicates a severe obsession. A person who has serious difficulties proving that he or she is alive or that other things are alive is known as a solipsist. This type of emotional psychological problem is rarely encountered in OCD, but it has been reported. It's not unusual, since the obsession may make you feel that your mind is being controlled.

78. *Sometimes I feel that there are no feelings, and that I cannot perceive my body parts as they are. Is that a symptom of OCD?* OCD does not engender these kinds of symptoms. Such symptoms are sometimes found in patients suffering from schizophrenia. Since OCD patients worry excessively, many times they may begin to question whether their perceptions are real, and some obsessions may incorrectly be perceived as psychotic.

79. *Am I free?* Life is very complicated today. Government, society, and family impose upon us an extraordinary number of demands. These demands include the expectation of growing up, going to school, studying, working, serving in the military, marrying, having children, paying taxes, being successful, being a good neighbor, preventing catastrophies, obtaining insurance, protecting our property, taking care of our health, lowering our cholesterol, and so forth. The list is extremely long, and facing these many demands is highly stressful. Since we live within the system, it becomes a highly complex matter to evade or escape from all these demands, and they become a daily burden. Certainly, if you have an obsessive-compulsive personality, you will have some difficulties remaining free, since you will feel compelled to abide by these demands. Since an obsessive-compulsive personality is already characterized by an "uptightness," which makes it difficult to relax, you will have to consider how you can overcome this oppressive life-style.

80. *Am I an OCD person?*   You are not an "OCD person"; you just have OCD. It is important to distinguish between being and having. If you were the illness, you couldn't get rid of it without getting rid of yourself. But if you have OCD, then you can get rid of it without disappearing in the process. This is an important factor because as part of our language we mistakenly describe our illness as a part of ourselves: in other words, we don't "have" an illness, we "are" the illness. By becoming the illness we lose our identity, will, and strength, and it becomes an uphill battle to fight back against any kind of disorder that may affect us.

81. *Are people who suffer from OCD "free"?*   Unfortunately, people suffering from OCD are not free. When the symptoms are very intense and invasive, the disorder takes over. Life becomes unbearable, and they become slaves to their illness.

82. *Is marital status affected by OCD?*   Yes. Marital status appears to be affected by OCD. In fact, more male patients suffering from OCD tend to remain single, as compared to women.

83. *Is there a relationship between occupation and OCD?*   A person's occupational status does not appear to be related to OCD. The disorder can be found in every social and economic layer.

84. *Are OCD and religious affiliation related?*   It seems that OCD might be seen more often among Protestants than among Catholics or Jews, but this may be the result of population distribution. Some research has indicated that certain religious groups might be more affected by OCD; nonetheless, this requires further clarification because the available data have not been confirmed.

85. *Is OCD hereditary?*   Studies that have investigated the presence of OCD in blood relatives are inconclusive. OCD is seen twice as much in mothers of OCD patients as in their fathers. Some genetic links have been found between OCD and Gilles de la Tourette's syndrome. There is no conclusive evidence that

OCD is inherited. More family constellation and genetic studies are needed.

86. *Are more women than men affected by this disorder?* Most studies appear to indicate that there is almost a one to one ratio between female and male OCD sufferers.

87. *At what age does OCD appear?* OCD may appear at any age, but it appears most often between the ages of three and thirty for women and three and twenty-one for men. It usually peaks in both sexes at about age eight.

88. *Does doubting create a problem?* Certainly. Doubting is a major problem and an obstacle to remaining free. Doubting was the name given to OCD over 100 years ago. It was called *folie de doute* (delusion of doubt) by the French. As long as we doubt, we cannot make decisions and carry on with our lives. We become dependent, and consequently we lose our freedom.

89. *Is fear of going blind a common symptom?* We have seen patients with this symptom. Any song, image, or person associated with blindness elicits fear of going blind. At times the fear may generalize to becoming deaf or handicapped.

90. *Is checking license plates common?* Some patients check for certain numbers or particular states on license plates. Sometimes they follow cars until they see another plate from the same state or the number adds up to the same total.

91. *What is hypermorality?* Hypermorality is an exaggerated moral sense—an overwhelming feeling of responsibility. Sometimes the word *scrupulosity* is used.

92. *Is hypermorality a symptom of OCD?* Yes. Many patients take pride in their exaggerated sense of morals. But the symptom is very often a nuisance to others. In addition, it is a symptom of the disorder and not a function of the superiority of the patients' values or morals.

93. *How does hypermorality manifest itself?* Patients who have this symptom may do the following:

Avoid picking up money lost by someone else

Refuse to go on disability because others may need it more

Seek unrelentingly the owner of an unimportant item in order to return it

Worry excessively about the possibility of hurting someone's feelings

Refuse to allow their self-employed spouses or parents to include them on their group medical insurance

If they break something in a store, immediately report it to the manager and insist on paying for it even if the store chooses to overlook it

Report to the IRS every cash dollar they earn, even if it adds up to only a few hundred dollars

Report cheating in the classroom

94. *Is the content of obsessions important?* Obsessions are becoming more important to behavioral therapists. In our latest research, we are beginning to isolate obsessions that respond to behavior therapy and those that don't.

95. *How common is the feeling of stickiness?* Some patients feel their hands are sticky, even when they are not. They have an urge to wash or avoid. Other times, when the average person could tolerate a little stickiness, the patient with OCD cannot. We have observed this in children as well as adults.

96. *Is kleptomania a form of OCD?* Kleptomania refers to the compulsion to steal something regardless of its value in an attempt to alleviate anxiety. This is a symptom of OCD. Patients who have this may get the urge anytime, and they will feel anxious until they steal. Very often, they are economically well off and can easily afford the item.

97. *Do children have a better treatment outcome?* Children are more difficult to treat because they do not follow instructions like adults. Behavioral therapy exercises must be presented to them very differently than to adults. The psychiatrist also has to be more careful in considering medication.

98.   *Do adolescents respond to treatments similarly to adults?*   No. Adolescence is a rough stage for anyone to go through. There are a host of emotions to deal with besides those created by OCD. Adolescents feel very angry, like "freaks," and are extremely ashamed. It is an age during which the individual has a strong need to be approved of by his or her peers, and OCD makes it very difficult. Adolescents often blame their parents for their problems, and their anger can severely disrupt family life.

99.   *Should families stop the compulsions?*   Family members should leave the house for a limited time while the patient performs the compulsion and/or asks for reassurance. Trying to stop the compulsion will increase anxiety, thereby increasing the compulsion itself. If the family members are asked by the patient and therapist to help prevent compulsions, then they can try to cajole the patient to stop. If it doesn't work, then leave the patient alone.

100.   *What is trichotillomania?*   Trichotillomania refers to patients' urge to pull their hair, eyebrows, eyelashes, and sometimes pubic hair. It is more common in women than men. Even very young children exhibit this behavior. It is treatable by both medication and behavior therapy.

Appendix A:
Social Readjustment
Rating Scale*

Instructions: Below is a list of events that you may have experienced during the past year. Please check off those events that did occur. Next to each event is a number. After you finish the questionnaire add up the numbers next to the event. If you score 300 or above it means you are very stressed. Scores between 150–300 indicate moderate stress. Below 150 indicates little stress.

Rank	Life Event	No. Value	
1	Death of spouse	100	____
2	Divorce	73	____
3	Marital separation	65	____
4	Jail term	63	____
5	Death of close family member	63	____
6	Personal injury or illness	53	____
7	Marriage	50	____
8	Fired at work	47	____
9	Marital reconciliation	45	____
10	Retirement	45	____
11	Change in health of family member	44	____
12	Pregnancy	40	____
13	Sex difficulties	39	____
14	Gain of new family member	39	____
15	Business readjustment	39	____
16	Change in financial state	38	____
17	Death of close friend	37	____
18	Change to different line of work	36	____

Rank	Life Event	No. Value	
19	Change in number of arguments with spouse	35	___
20	Mortgage over $100,000	31	___
21	Foreclosure on mortgage or loan	30	___
22	Change in responsibilities at work	29	___
23	Son or daughter leaving home	29	___
24	Trouble with in-laws	29	___
25	Outstanding personal achievement	28	___
26	Wife begin or stop work	26	___
27	Begin or end school	26	___
28	Change in living conditions	25	___
29	Revision of personal habits	24	___
30	Trouble with boss	23	___
31	Change in work hours or conditions	20	___
32	Change in residence	20	___
33	Change in schools	20	___
34	Change in recreation	19	___
35	Change in church activities	19	___
36	Change in social activities	18	___
37	Mortgage or loan less than $100,000	17	___
38	Change in sleeping habits	16	___
39	Change in number of family get togethers	15	___
40	Change in eating habits	15	___
41	Vacation	13	___
42	Christmas	12	___
43	Minor violations of the law	11	___
	Total score:		___

*From *Journal of Psychosomatic Research* by Thomas H. Holmes and Richard H. Rahe, 1967.

Appendix B: Guidelines for Families Coping with Obsessive-Compulsive Disorder

1. Keep cool at home. Use a quiet manner.

2. Lower expectations temporarily. Compare progress this month to last month, rather than last year or next year. Patients' progress must be compared to themselves, not others.

3. Overlook rituals and checking. See these as coping strategies. Don't participate in rituals.

4. Don't be judgmental of the behavior. Accept it as the best the patient can do right now.

5. Do not pressure the patient to verbalize anxiety (it only makes matters worse).

6. Help channel energy into activities such as jogging, swimming, and dancing. Activity is more likely to calm the patient down than talking it out.

7. Allow verbal expression of rage and anger. Listen to what the patient says. Try not to be defensive.

8. Help the patient develop confidence in his or her own decisions and choices by allowing him or her enough time to make them. Never make decisions for another person (unless a young child) but help the person to make them.

9. Do not confront the patient with what he or she says or does. Reflect on the feelings behind the action and allow for further discussion.

10. Do not pressure the patient to stop compulsions, but stick to the time allocated by the therapist. If the patient is not in therapy, then cut down slowly on the time of the activity.

11. Always explain changes. Make only reasonable demands.

12. Limits calm things down. Everyone needs to know what the rules are. Set limits on the amount of time he or she talks beyond ten minutes. Conversation beyond ten minutes may not be productive. Do not restrict rituals.

13. Ignore what you can't change. Let some things slide. Never ignore violence or suicidal threats.

14. Say what you have to say clearly, calmly, and in a positive way.

15. Follow doctor's orders. Medications should be taken as prescribed. Only medications that are prescribed should be taken.

16. Carry on business as usual. Reconnect with friends, hobbies, and family routines.

17. Look out for street drugs or alcohol. They make symptoms worse.

18. Pick up on early changes and signs and consult with the patient's therapist and/or doctor.

19. Solve problems step by step. Make changes gradually. Work on one thing at a time.

20. Don't get involved in the behavioral modification program unless asked to do so by the patient and his or her therapist.

Index

About the Authors

FUGEN NEZIROGLU, PH.D., is a behavior therapist who has been involved in the research of obsessive-compulsive disorder for over fifteen years. She received her Ph.D. in both clinical and school-community psychology from Hofstra University. She has done postgraduate work in behavior therapy and is a diplomate both in clinical and in behavioral psychology. For over ten years, she has been an assistant professor teaching graduate courses in the department of psychology at Hofstra University.

Both a scientist and a practitioner, Dr. Neziroglu has presented or published over seventy-five papers in scientific journals and books, and is co-author with Dr. Yaryura-Tobias of a book entitled *Obsessive-Compulsive Disorder: Pathogenesis, Diagnosis, and Treatment* (New York: Marcel Dekker, 1983). Dr. Neziroglu believes in the integration of the biological and behavioral approaches to the disorder.

Dr. Neziroglu is also clinical director of Bio-Behavioral Psychiatry, where she provides direct services, supervises all psychology interns, sponsors many doctoral dissertations, and conducts research. She is a member of many national and international societies and is on the scientific advisory board of the Obsessive-Compulsive Foundation.

JOSE A. YARYURA-TOBIAS, M.D., F.A.C.N., is a biological psychiatrist and internist with over thirty years of experience. He is also a writer and a poet. He received his medical degree at the National University of Buenos Aires and completed internships in Argentina, Canada, and the United States, originally specializing in medicine. He later took a second residency to pursue research in biological psychiatry.

Dr. Yaryura-Tobias has pioneered research in the dopamine theory of schizophrenia and the biological theory of obessive-compulsive disorder. He is co-author of a book with Dr. Neziroglu entitled *Obessive-Compulsive Disorder: Pathogenesis, Diagnosis, and Treatment* (New York: Marcel Dekker, 1983) and is also author of *The Integral Being* (New York: Henry Holt & Co., 1987). He has presented or published over 150 scientific papers.

Dr. Yaryura-Tobias has served as professor of psychopharmacology at the J.F. Kennedy University in Buenos Aires. He is currently a member of numerous national and international societies and a founding member of the International College of Psychosomatic Medicine, the Argentine Society of Biological Psychiatry, the World Federation of Biological Psychiatry, and the Society of Obsessive-Compulsive Disorders. He is also a fellow of the American College of Nutrition and serves on the scientific advisory board of the Obsessive-Compulsive Foundation.